I0831065

TAPAS ESPAÑA

70 Easy Recipes for Gathering and Sharing

CATHERINE COGLIANDRO ALIOTO
Photography by Erin Scott

weldonowen

CONTENTS

INTRODUCTION

Tapas, simple plates of shared dishes, originated in Spain and are more than just a way of eating; they are an integral part of Spanish culture. These small, flavorful dishes are shared among friends and family in a communal setting, making for a convivial social experience, with "little bites" of tasty, varied dishes enjoyed in a relaxing, unhurried way. Typically served in cafés and bars throughout the country, tapas range from simple dishes of just a few ingredients to sophisticated flavor and ingredient combinations. Tapas are popular with home cooks, too, both for everyday meals and for entertaining. Because so many tapas can be prepared in advance, hosts can relax and visit with their guests while enjoying delicious appetizers together.

It is believed that the Arabs from North Africa brought their tradition of eating small plates of food, called *mezze*, to the Andalusian region of southern Spain, and in doing so, influenced the cuisine. Tapas means "to cover," and originally referred to the small plates of bread or cheese provided to customers to cover their glasses of sherry in the hot, insect-filled bars of Andalusia. The custom spread to other regions of the country, with each region eventually developing its own traditions and specialties. What were at first simple offerings of snacks evolved over the years into delicious, varied foods ranging from nibbles (*cosas de picar*), such as salted almonds and warm olives, to skewered bites (*banderillas*) to complex casseroles and stews (*cazuelas*).

Tapas highlight the abundant and delicious ingredients available throughout Spain, ingredients that came from around the globe. The Romans introduced olives to Spain, and the Arabs brought rice, citrus, almonds, and sugar. Spanish explorers returned from the New World with previously unknown foods such as potatoes, tomatoes, corn, avocado, papaya, peppers, and cacao. Spain is also rich in spices, such as saffron and *pimentón*, a result of seven hundred years of Arab occupation of the Iberian Peninsula. And, given that Spain is surrounded on three sides by water, including the Mediterranean Sea and the Atlantic Ocean, seafood is central to its cuisine.

In Spain, it's common for groups of friends to travel from bar to bar enjoying as many as six to eight tapas dishes before dinner, a custom that is referred to as *tapear*. Because the portions are quite small, guests can enjoy a variety of dishes before their main meal. For those who want larger portions or a full meal, *raciones* are also on offer. Whether in the northern Basque city of San Sebastián or the southern cities of Málaga and Granada, "tapas tours" are commonplace. A complete tapas experience would include a selection of restaurants, each highlighting its own specialties. With the recipes in this book, you can create your own tapas tour right at home!

HOW TO USE THIS BOOK

This book is organized by types of tapas, beginning with nibbles designed to be served alongside a glass of wine, to those fried, speared, served on bread, or encased in dough, followed by more substantial dishes with meats and rice. The book finishes with a selection of traditional Spanish desserts. Each recipe is designed to be served in small portions, but should you prefer to serve something as a main dish, such as a paella, it's simply a matter of presentation.

The recipes attempt to highlight the incredible assortment of ingredients available in Spain and typically and traditionally used in Spanish cooking. The recipes reflect traditions and specialties of each region. In the Basque region of Northern Spain, the food is heavily influenced by its proximity to France. It is the center of the fishing industry and many dishes are made with a *pisto*, which is a combination of sautéed onions, peppers, and tomatoes. In San Sebastián, located in the Basque Country, tapas are called *pintxos*, or *pinchos*, after the pick/skewer on which they are served. The name comes from *pinchar*, meaning "to pinch" or "to poke." San Sebastián is known for its tapas bars, where they serve bite-size tapas on bread or speared with a toothpick.

At tapas bars in the north, the varied tapas are displayed on the counter, ranging from cold to hot dishes, large and small. Here, cider and white wines, such as Albariño and Txakoli, are the preferred drink. Andalusia and Southern Spain offer an abundance of fish, often fried. Sherry is their preferred drink. Seville, Andalusia, in particular, is home of the tapas. It is customary when arriving at a tapas bar to first order a glass of wine. The restaurant will then select a few dishes at random to go with your choice of drink. Catalans are known for their use of saffron, empanadas, and rich meat stews cooked in *cazuelas* and, of course, Cava—Spanish sparkling wine. Valencia is known for its paella and rice dishes.

We hope this book inspires you to cook, gather, and embrace the style of eating enjoyed throughout Spain.

¡Buen provecho!

To a delicious meal! Enjoy!

ARV
UM
LOUIT FRERES
DIJON
strong
MUSTARD
CENTO
ORGANIC
CHIQUILÍN
ORTIZ DESDE 1891 ORTIZ DESDE 1891
JO
SE
LIMÃO
in Olive Oil
ORTIZ
Anchovies

THE SPANISH PANTRY

Spanish food is considered the food of the people. The tapas in this book highlight the abundance of Spanish ingredients, most of which are readily available at your local grocery store, or online. The key to fully enjoying the informal and communal style of eating tapas, and the simplicity of their preparation, is to have a pantry stocked with an assortment of ingredients that can be easily plated or combined with fresh ingredients. Listed below are suggestions for some items to have on hand.

ANCHOVIES

Eaten fried, grilled, cured, and pickled. *Boquerones* refer to anchovies that are vinegar-cured and *anchoas* are anchovies that are salt-cured.

CHEESE

Cheeses of every type are available in Spain, made from sheep's, cow's, and goat's milks.

Manchego: One of the most familiar of Spanish cheeses, it is made from the flavorful milk of the Manchega sheep, which graze the rolling hills of La Mancha. Sheep's milk cheese contains twice the amount of butterfat as cow- or goat-milk cheeses. As Manchego ages, it becomes more salty, crumbly, and oily.

Mahón: A hard cow's milk cheese from the Mediterranean island of Minorca, available both fresh and aged. It has a pale-yellow color and a mild, dry, and gamey flavor. When aged, its texture resembles Parmesan, with an intense caramelized saltiness. It is piquant, buttery, and nutty, making it a versatile cheese that can be eaten plain or cooked. It can also substitute for Gouda and pairs well with chorizo, sherry, dried fruit, and nuts.

Idiazabal: A dense, dry, and nutty cheese made from the milk of the Laxta sheep in the Pyrenees. It pairs well with crisp apples and ham and with quince and walnuts.

Tetilla: A soft cheese from Galicia known for its creamy consistency.

Cabrales: A blue cheese matured in limestone caves, with a strong pungent nose and a complex flavor profile.

Murcia al Vino (Drunken goat cheese): A flavorful goat cheese from southeastern Spain notable for its wine-soaked rind.

FISH

Canned tuna is one of the most consumed fishes in the world. Its flavor is exceptional, and it is high in omega-3 fatty acids and protein, as well as B vitamins and minerals, such as iron, magnesium, and phosphorus. It is also known to lower cholesterol and prevents and fights diseases such as anemia. Tuna is a staple of Spanish cuisine, and Spain has a long history of traditional fishing using the *almadraba* method of net-fishing. The Spanish enjoy tuna in many forms, and they particularly enjoy the prized *ventresca* (tuna belly), which is highly regarded for its quality and taste. Regions such as Andalusia are well-known for their tuna dishes.

LEGUMES

Beans and chickpeas are the most consumed foods in Spain after bread.

MEATS

Jamón: *Jamón ibérico de bellota* is dry-cured ham of either the black Iberian pigs who graze the wild pastures of southwestern Spain eating acorns (*bellotas*) and grass, or a fifty-fifty mixture of the Iberian and Duroc pigs. The ham, which has a high fat content and is rich in flavor, is a mainstay of Spanish cuisine.

Beef, Pork, and Lamb: The Spanish prefer veal and pig roasted, grilled, or sautéed in a sauce. Roasted meats are traditionally served on holidays and festive occasions.

Chicken: Chicken is very popular in Spain and is typically prepared fried or stewed.

Chorizo: This pork sausage is made with paprika, which gives it its distinctive red color. Available both fresh and soft and smoked and aged.

MEMBRILLO

A sweet paste made from quince. It pairs well with hard cheeses, such as Manchego.

NUTS

Spain is one of the top producers of almonds, hazelnuts, and walnuts. Almond trees are native to the Middle East and Asia and were likely brought to Spain by the Romans and have been thriving throughout Spain for more than two thousand years. The trees, and their blossoms, are a symbol of love and beauty. Many Spanish recipes of Arabic origin contain ground almonds. Almonds are also used to make a *picada* (a mixture of garlic, parsley, and nuts), which is essential to Catalan and Valencian cuisine.

NORA PEPPERS

Nora peppers, also known as ball peppers for their round shape, are grown in Valencia and add a beautiful red color and sweet, intense flavor to paella and romesco sauce. These are most often available as dried chiles. To use, remove the stem, cut in half, and discard the seeds, which are bitter. Soak in cold water until soft. Remove the skin and add to your dish. Ancho peppers are a suitable substitute.

OLIVES

Spain is the largest producer of olives in the world, mostly coming from the province of Andalusia. In ancient Rome, olives were synonymous with wealth. They are often marinated with garlic, herbs, onion, or citrus and served warm, or occasionally stuffed with anchovies or pimientos.

PAPRIKA/PIMENTÓN

A spice made from sweet red peppers and available in sweet, spicy, and smoky flavors. Paprika gives Spanish chorizo its distinctive red color and smoky flavor.

PEDRO XIMÉNEZ BALSAMIC VINEGAR

A vinegar made from Andalusian fortified wine. The grapes are often dried in the sun to concentrate the sugars.

PIMENT D'ESPELETTE

A chile pepper grown exclusively in the Basque village of Espelette, it is known for its complex flavor profile of smoky, sweet, and fruity. It was originally brought to Spain from Mexico in the sixteenth century. The government limits its export, making it rare and expensive outside of France. It can be found online and at specialty food shops. Substitute Spanish paprika or a pinch of cayenne pepper.

SAFFRON

Saffron, called *azafrán* in Spanish, is the Arab word for yellow, the color it lends to food. The threads are the dried stigmas from the purple crocus plant, and each is picked by hand. It is the world's most expensive spice. La Mancha produces some of the finest saffron in the world. For the best quality, always purchase the whole threads and not a powder, which can sometimes be mixed with turmeric. To bring out the aroma and flavor of the saffron threads, pulverize a few stands in a mortar and pestle, then place in a bowl with a few teaspoons of warm liquid to bloom before adding to a dish.

SHERRY VINEGAR

Sherry vinegar comes from sherry, a fortified wine made in the Jerez region of Spain. The vinegar is aged in oak barrels, giving it a deep, tangy and slightly sweet flavor. It is used in dishes throughout Spain. Sherry vinegar will keep for up to six months in a cool, dark place.

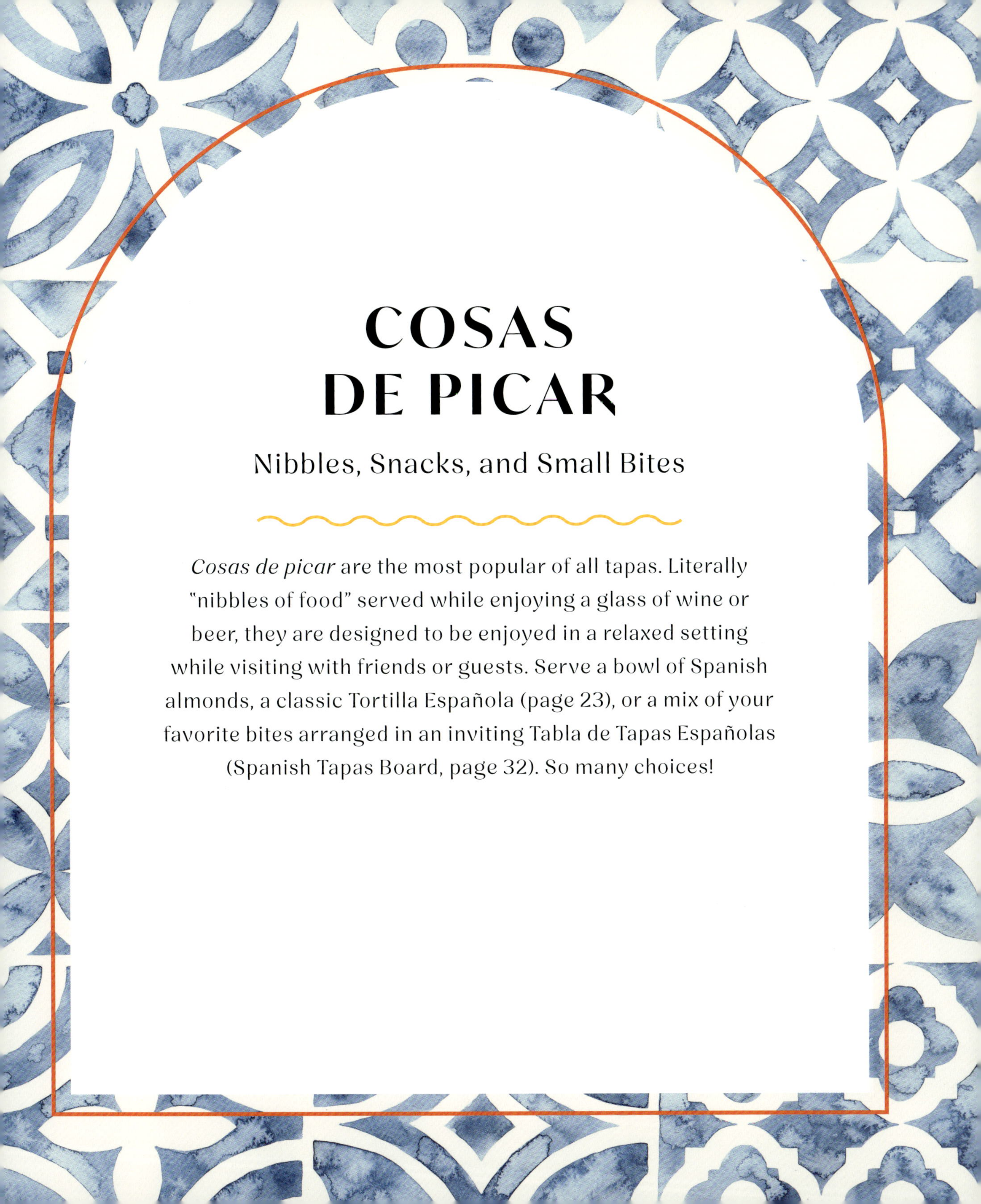

COSAS DE PICAR

Nibbles, Snacks, and Small Bites

Cosas de picar are the most popular of all tapas. Literally "nibbles of food" served while enjoying a glass of wine or beer, they are designed to be enjoyed in a relaxed setting while visiting with friends or guests. Serve a bowl of Spanish almonds, a classic Tortilla Española (page 23), or a mix of your favorite bites arranged in an inviting Tabla de Tapas Españolas (Spanish Tapas Board, page 32). So many choices!

ESCALIVADA

Olive-Oil Roasted Vegetables

Escalivada is a traditional dish popular in Catalonia, Valencia, Murcia, and Aragon. "*Escalibar*" in Catalan means to "cook in ashes," referencing the traditional preparation of the dish where the vegetables are cooked over hot embers on a grill. Alternatively, the vegetables can be cooked indoors in an oven.

Escalivada is a dish of grilled vegetables, typically peppers, eggplant, onions, and garlic, that are charred, giving the vegetables a smoky, sweet flavor. Considered the Catalan version of ratatouille, it is usually served chilled or at room temperature, with Coca (page 27), a flatbread similar to pizza; on Pan con Tomate (page 26); or alongside Tortilla Española (page 23). It is also delicious served as a relish with grilled meats or fish.

For best results, the vegetables should be cooked separately, as each requires different cooking times. It is also important not to overcrowd the pans, as this will result in the vegetable steaming instead of roasting.

VEGETABLES

2 red bell peppers, halved and seeded

2 Roma tomatoes

1 eggplant, pierced with a fork

1 red onion, unpeeled

1 bulb of garlic, top trimmed to expose the cloves

½ cup olive oil

VINAIGRETTE

3 tablespoons extra-virgin olive oil

1 tablespoon sherry vinegar

1 tablespoon finely chopped fresh parsley

Salt and freshly ground pepper

YIELD 4 TO 6 SERVINGS

Preheat the oven to 425°F.

To roast the vegetables: Lay out two baking sheets. On one, place the bell peppers and tomatoes. On the other, the eggplant, onion, and garlic. Coat all the vegetables well with the olive oil. Place in the oven and roast until the vegetables are charred and soft, 10 to 20 minutes for the bell peppers and tomatoes and 35 to 45 minutes for the eggplant, onion, and garlic. Let cool, then peel each of the vegetables and slice them into long strips and squeeze the cloves from the garlic.

To make the vinaigrette: In a small bowl, whisk together the extra-virgin olive oil, vinegar, and parsley. Season to taste with salt and pepper.

Combine the bell peppers, tomatoes, eggplant, onion, and garlic cloves in a large bowl and toss well with the vinaigrette, adjusting the seasonings, if needed. Set aside for at least an hour, allowing the flavors to blend.

The vegetables will keep in an airtight container in the refrigerator for up to 1 week.

CEVICHE DE CAMARONES

Prawn Ceviche

This ceviche is cooked in an acidic sauce and served chilled, making it an ideal dish for the warm summer months. The prawns are best served with *tortas de aceite* (olive oil crackers). Look for brands such as Ines Rosales, which can usually be found in specialty markets and online.

1 cup dry white wine, such as Albariño

3 sprigs fresh thyme, plus 1 teaspoon finely chopped leaves

1 pound medium prawns, peeled and deveined

½ medium red onion, peeled and thinly sliced

½ cucumber, peeled, seeded, and diced

2 tablespoons fresh lemon juice

2 tablespoons fresh orange juice

2 tablespoons finely chopped fresh parsley

1 tablespoon olive oil

¼ teaspoon kosher salt

¼ teaspoon red pepper flakes

YIELD 4 SERVINGS

In a large saucepan, bring the wine and 1 cup water to a boil over high heat. Add the thyme sprigs and reduce the heat to a simmer. Add the prawns and gently poach until opaque and slightly pink, 2 to 3 minutes. Using a slotted spoon, transfer the prawns to a medium bowl and gently stir in the onion, cucumber, lemon juice, orange juice, parsley, oil, salt, and red pepper flakes. Discard the poaching liquid.

Refrigerate for 1 hour to allow the prawns to absorb the flavors of the marinade.

Serve in four individual bowls.

GARBANZONS CRUJIENTES CON PIMENTÓN

Crispy Pimento Chickpeas

These protein-rich chickpeas make a satisfying and nutritious snack on their own. Crunchy, salty, and smoky, these little nibbles are also the perfect addition to a tapas board and a great topping for a mixed green salad.

One 15-ounce can garbanzo beans (chickpeas), drained and rinsed

1 to 2 tablespoons extra-virgin olive oil

Kosher salt

Smoked paprika for seasoning

YIELD 1 CUP

Preheat the oven to 425°F. Line a baking sheet with parchment paper.

In a medium bowl, gently toss together the beans, oil, and salt to taste until well combined. Spread them evenly on the prepared baking sheet and roast until toasted and golden, about 20 minutes. Cool slightly, then transfer to a bowl and toss with the paprika to taste. Serve at room temperature.

The toasted garbanzo beans will keep in an airtight container at room temperature for up to 1 week.

PIMIENTOS DE PADRÓN

Padrón Peppers with Coarse Salt

Padrón peppers are native to Galicia, an autonomous community in the far northwest of Spain. These small, vibrant-green peppers are typically mild and earthy in flavor, but every now and then, you'll encounter one with the heat equivalent of a jalapeño. The delicious flavor of the peppers makes them a favorite tapa in Spain. The possibility of a spicy bite just adds to their appeal!

1 tablespoon neutral oil, such as sunflower oil

1 pound Padrón peppers, rinsed

1 teaspoon coarse salt

Drizzle of olive oil

YIELD 2 CUPS

In a medium sauté pan or skillet, heat the neutral oil over medium heat. Add the peppers to the pan, arranging them in a single layer and cook, without stirring, until the skins are charred, 5 to 7 minutes. Transfer to a bowl to serve, sprinkling them with the salt to taste and a drizzle of olive oil.

Store leftover peppers in an airtight container in the refrigerator for 3 to 4 days.

Spanish Padron peppers (pimiento de Padron) *are from the region of Galicia, in a town called Padron, where they were first grown by Franciscan monks in the sixteenth century. It is believed that the monks brought the seeds back to Spain from Central America or Mexico. Padron peppers tend to be sweet and mild, although occasionally you'll surprised by one that's fairly spicy. The hot climate and arid conditions in which they are grown determine the heat of the peppers. They are easy to prepare; simply char in a heavy pan with a bit of oil, or over a grill. To serve, place the peppers in a bowl and sprinkle with a flaky salt, such as Maldon, which adds flavor and a nice crunch.*

FLAT FILLETS OF
ANCHOVIES
IN OLIVE OIL

TORTILLA ESPAÑOLA

Spanish Tortilla

Not to be confused with the Mexican tortilla, *tortilla Española*, or *tortilla de patatas*, is a Spanish version of a frittata made with creamy potatoes gently cooked with eggs, olive oil, and paprika. It is one of Spain's most beloved and well-known dishes, made regularly by home cooks and a ubiquitous staple at tapas bars throughout the country. It can be eaten for breakfast, lunch, or dinner.

For best results, use a waxy potato, such as Yukon gold, which will hold its shape without falling apart during cooking. The recipe calls for plenty of olive oil, so the potatoes are essentially poached, resulting in a frittata with a creamy interior and soft, flavorful exterior.

The dish can be served warm or cold, cut into wedges and eaten alongside a salad or on its own, or atop a piece of toasted bread as a *montadito* (mini open-faced sandwich).

---

8 large eggs

1 teaspoon smoked paprika

3 teaspoons kosher salt

½ cup olive oil, plus more as needed

1 onion, thinly sliced

1 pound Yukon gold potato, sliced into thin rounds

1½ teaspoons freshly ground pepper

YIELD ONE 8-INCH TORTILLA

In a large bowl, whisk the eggs and paprika with 1 teaspoon of the salt until frothy. Set aside.

In an 8-inch nonstick sauté pan or skillet, warm the ½ cup of oil over medium heat. Add the onion and potatoes and season with the remaining 2 teaspoons salt and the pepper. Cook, stirring occasionally, until the potatoes are fork-tender, 15 to 20 minutes. Using a slotted spoon, transfer the onion and potato mixture to the bowl of eggs and, with a rubber spatula, gently combine. Reserve the oil.

Over medium heat, warm the reserved oil and add the onion, potato, and egg mixture to the pan. Continue to cook while gently swirling the pan until the eggs begin to set, 5 to 10 minutes. Reduce the heat, if necessary, to prevent the bottom of the tortilla from becoming too brown.

Circle a rubber spatula around the edges of the pan to help loosen and shape the tortilla. Remove from the heat and place a large plate over the top of the pan. Quickly invert the tortilla onto the plate. If needed, add another 1 tablespoon oil to the pan and slide the tortilla back into the pan, cooking over medium heat for 3 to 5 minutes until fully set and golden brown.

To serve, slide the tortilla onto a clean plate and cut it into wedges. Alternatively, it can be cut into cubes and served as a *pintxo* (little skewer) on a piece of toasted baguette.

Leftover tortilla will keep in an airtight container in the refrigerator for up to 3 days.

HUEVOS RELLENOS CON PIMENTÓN

Deviled Eggs with Paprika

Stuffed, or deviled, eggs have been a part of Spanish cuisine since the thirteenth century, particularly in Andalusia. Easy to prepare ahead of time, this recipe calls for sweet paprika to add a pop of color and flavor. Feel free to experiment with other toppings, for instance, crisp slivers of *jamón serrano* or chopped chives.

---

3 large eggs

1 tablespoon mayonnaise

¼ teaspoon Dijon mustard

¼ teaspoon sweet paprika

Pinch of kosher salt

2 tablespoons minced fresh parsley

YIELD 6 SERVINGS

Place the eggs in a small saucepan and cover by 2 inches of cold water. Bring the water to a boil over medium-high heat. Remove from the heat, cover, and let sit for 10 minutes. Using a slotted spoon, transfer the eggs from the pan to a bowl of ice water to chill for 5 minutes. Drain and peel.

Slice the eggs in half lengthwise and gently pop out the yolks. Set the whites aside.

In a small bowl, mash together the yolks, mayonnaise, mustard, paprika, and salt until smooth. Gently spoon the filling into the egg halves, mounding slightly. Garnish with parsley and serve.

Store finished deviled eggs in an airtight container in the refrigerator for 2 to 3 days.

PAN CON TOMATE/PA AMB TOMÀQUET

Catalan Garlic Bread

Pan con tomate, or *pa amb tomàquet* in Catalan, is the humblest of all tapas. It originated in Catalonia and is typically served at tapas bars as a free snack. This recipe uses tomato pulp, not diced or sliced tomatoes. Another option is to make a tomato *concasse* by peeling, seeding, and chopping the tomatoes before combining them with oil, minced garlic, and salt and spooning the mixture onto toasted bread.

In tapas bars, the *pan con tomate* is often topped with an anchovy or a slice of Manchego cheese. For maximum flavor, use tomatoes that are at their peak, toward the end of summer.

1 loaf ciabatta, sliced crosswise into 1½-inch-wide slices

Extra-virgin olive oil for drizzling

2 cloves garlic, peeled

2 large tomatoes, halved

Coarse salt

YIELD 4 TO 6 SERVINGS

Preheat the broiler.

Drizzle the bread slices with the oil and toast under the broiler, or on a griddle over high heat, until golden brown and crisp. Rub each slice well with the garlic and then a tomato half until the pulp has generously coated the bread. Discard the skin. Sprinkle with salt and transfer to a plate to enjoy.

COCA

Spanish Flatbread

Coca is a flatbread from Barcelona and is known as Catalonia's answer to pizza. Its thin, crunchy crust can serve as an accompaniment to a variety of tapas or it can hold any number of toppings, although never cheese and rarely tomatoes. Some historians believe that *coca* was the precursor to the Italian pizza and was introduced to Naples when it was conquered by Spain.

A sweet version of *coca* is traditionally enjoyed around the holidays and is served at breakfast or for dessert with tea or sweet wine.

---

1 tablespoon active dry yeast

1 cup warm water

Pinch of sugar

1⅔ cups all-purpose flour, plus more as needed

½ teaspoon kosher salt

¼ cup olive oil, plus more for the bowl and pan

YIELD ONE 9-BY-13-INCH FLATBREAD

Preheat the oven to 450°F.

In a small bowl, combine the yeast and warm water and sprinkle in the sugar. Leave until frothy, about 10 minutes, then set aside.

In the bowl of a stand mixer fitted with the whisk attachment, whisk together the flour, salt, and oil. Switch to the dough hook, set the mixer to medium speed, and add the yeast mixture. Knead until the dough is smooth and elastic, 2 to 3 minutes, scraping down the sides of the bowl and adding a little more flour, if needed.

Form the dough into a ball and place in a large, lightly oiled bowl. Cover with plastic wrap and let stand in a warm place until the dough puffs slightly, about 30 minutes.

Lightly oil a 9-by-13-inch rimmed baking sheet. Using your hands, gently press the dough evenly into the pan, including the edges.

Bake until the edges begin to brown, about 25 minutes. Remove from the oven and cool slightly. Cut into pieces and enjoy plain or with your favorite toppings.

Store at room temperature, wrapped tightly in plastic wrap. For longer storage, freeze the cooled bread wrapped tightly in plastic wrap and then placed in a freezer-safe bag. Thaw at room temperature before serving.

CIE DE

PICOS
Breadsticks

Serve these crunchy breadsticks alongside your tapas platter or eat them on their own as a snack. Feel free to flavor them with 1 teaspoon of chopped fresh herbs, such as rosemary, or 1 tablespoon grated Manchego cheese or freshly ground black pepper. Add the flavorings along with the flour.

---

1 teaspoon active dry yeast

½ cup warm water

Pinch of sugar

1 cup all-purpose flour

1 teaspoon kosher salt

1 tablespoon olive oil, plus more for the bowl

YIELD 6 PICOS

In a small bowl, combine the yeast and warm water and sprinkle in the sugar. Set aside until the mixture begins to froth, 5 to 10 minutes.

In the bowl of a stand mixer fitted with a dough hook, combine the yeast mixture, flour, salt, and oil. Mix on medium speed until the dough is smooth, 5 to 7 minutes. Remove from the mixer, form the dough into a ball, and place it in a bowl coated with the olive oil. Cover the bowl with plastic wrap and set aside to rest, about 30 minutes.

Preheat the oven to 400°F.

Remove the dough from the bowl and cut it evenly into six pieces. Shape each piece into a 6-inch-long rope. Place the ropes on a baking sheet, spacing them a few inches apart. Let rest for another 30 minutes.

Transfer the baking sheet to the oven and bake for 20 minutes until the breadsticks are golden and crisp.

Picos will keep in a tightly sealed container at room temperature for up to 1 week.

ACEITUNAS CALIENTES CON NARANJA Y HOJUELAS DE CHILE

Warm Olives with Orange and Chili Flakes

Most Spanish olives are grown in the Andalusia region of Spain, where the majority is pressed into oil. It is believed that the Phoenicians introduced olive trees to Spain more than three thousand years ago.

These fragrant and flavorful olives are irresistible. Use a variety of cured olives, ranging in color and texture, including the fruity green arbequina and a high-quality olive oil. Serve warm.

1 cup assorted olives
Three 2-inch strips orange peel
⅓ cup extra-virgin olive oil
2 cloves garlic, crushed
4 sprigs fresh thyme
Pinch of red pepper flakes

YIELD 1 CUP

In a small saucepan over medium heat, combine the olives, orange peel, oil, garlic, thyme, and red pepper flakes. Cook, stirring occasionally, for 2 minutes. Reduce the heat to low and cook, stirring occasionally, for 5 additional minutes.

Remove from the heat, and, using a slotted spoon, transfer the olives to a small bowl. The olives will keep, covered in oil and refrigerated, for up to 4 weeks.

TABLA DE TAPAS ESPAÑOLAS

Spanish Tapas Board

Featuring citrus-infused olives, Manchego cheese, *jamón serrano*, and a variety of other Spanish delicacies, this bountiful spread will transport you to a tapas bar in Spain.

Serve the tapas with a pitcher of cold sangria (see pages 140 and 143) and plenty of crackers or slices of rustic country bread. For an authentic Spanish experience, add *tortas de aceite* (crispy, sweet, olive oil crackers) to the platter. Find these in Spanish specialty stores or online.

Citrus-infused olives (see page 30), or olives of your choice

1 wedge plain Manchego cheese or cubes of Manchego cheese marinated in olive oil, red pepper flakes, and fresh herbs

Thin slices *jamón serrano*

Cured Spanish chorizo, cut into ½-inch pieces

Marcona almonds of your choice (salted, smoked, or flavored with herbs; see opposite)

Fresh or dried figs or fig jam

***Membrillo* (quince paste)**

Plenty of crackers or rustic country bread slices

***Tortas de aceite* (optional)**

Cold sangria, served in a pitcher

YIELD 6 TO 8 SERVINGS

Artfully arrange the ingredients on a wooden cheese board or in serving dishes of your choice.

Here are some suggestions for creating a tapas board:

- Olives, Marcona almonds, wedge of cheese or slices of sausage
- Assorted cheeses—see ingredients section for options
- Different sausages with *jamón* and cheeses
- Manchego plancha with sliced *membrillo* and drizzled with honey
- Cubes of Manchego marinated in olive oil, red pepper flakes, and herbs
- Manchego with fresh figs and cured chorizo
- Manchego fresco on toast with sliced green olives
- Skewers of grilled shrimp with aioli

ALMENDRAS ESPAÑOLAS

Spanish Almonds with Rosemary

These almonds are so quick and simple to prepare and make a delicious snack on their own or as a salty addition to any tapas board.

1½ teaspoons olive oil

1½ teaspoons chopped fresh rosemary leaves

1½ cups blanched whole almonds

1 tablespoon kosher salt

1½ teaspoons smoked paprika

YIELD 1½ CUPS

In a medium sauté pan or skillet, warm the oil over medium heat and add the rosemary, allowing it to perfume the oil for 1 to 2 minutes. Add the almonds and warm for 3 to 5 minutes until golden. Transfer to a bowl and toss with the salt and paprika. Serve warm.

After the almonds cool completely, store in an airtight container in a cool, dark, dry place. At room temperature, these almonds should remain fresh for 3 to 4 weeks; in a refrigerator, up to 1 year.

Almonds

Almonds were introduced to Spain by the Arabs, which is why many recipes of Arabic origin contain almonds.

Spain is one of world's top producers of almonds, and they grow well in its warm climate.

Spanish almonds refer to a variety of almonds grown in Spain, including the Marcona almond.

The Marcona almond is native to the Spanish Mediterranean. The are often referred to as the "queen of almonds," and they are enjoyed around the world. They are plumper in shape, creamier in texture, and sweeter and richer in flavor than typical almonds. They have a higher oil content, which gives them a slightly oily texture. Typically sautéed in oil and seasoned with salt and herbs, they are commonly eaten as a snack, often accompanying cheeses and meats as part of a tapas platter.

Spanish almonds have an elongated shape, and they are firmer in texture and milder in flavor. They are commonly used in a variety of savory and sweet dishes such as a picada, romesco, and turron.

PINTXOS, BANDERILLAS, Y PALILLOS

Skewers and Brochettes

Throughout Spain, skewered tapas are known by different names, depending on the region. In the Basque Country, they are called *pintxos*, pronounced "pinchos," meaning foods that are "stabbed" with toothpicks or skewers. In Northern Spain, the word *banderillas* refers to pickled vegetables, fish, or olives that are skewered, because the skewers resemble the *banderillas*, or darts, thrust at a bull during a bullfight. Another name for a skewered tapa is *palillo,* Spanish for "toothpick."

All of these skewered, spiked, or speared tapas can be made in advance, often with ingredients readily found in the pantry or refrigerator. They can vary from a simple cube of cheese skewered with a slice of apple to a more sophisticated pairing, such as marinated and grilled meats interlaced with peppers or pineapple. Create a variety of *pintxos* by combining different flavors, colors, and textures.

SANDIA Y QUESO DE CABRO CERRÓN

Watermelon and Goat Cheese

The sweet and juicy flavors of the watermelon perfectly complement the tangy goat cheese. The watermelon and cheese should be cut into bite-size cubes. To enjoy as the Spanish do, put the entire tapa in your mouth at once.

2 tablespoons olive oil

1 teaspoon Pedro Ximénez balsamic vinegar, or similar high-quality balsamic vinegar

1 teaspoon minced fresh oregano leaves

½ teaspoon kosher salt

¼ teaspoon freshly ground pepper

¼ teaspoon sweet paprika

8 ounces watermelon, cut into ½-inch cubes

8 ounces Cerrón fresco goat cheese, cut into ½-inch cubes

YIELD 8 TO 12 SKEWERS

In a large bowl, whisk together the oil, vinegar, oregano, salt, pepper, and paprika. Add the watermelon and cheese cubes and gently toss to coat. Let marinate for 1 hour in the refrigerator. To serve, skewer one piece of watermelon and one piece of cheese on an antipasto skewer or toothpick. Repeat for the remaining fruit and cheese. Arrange on a platter and serve.

PIQUILLOS RELLENOS DE CANGREJO

Crab-Stuffed Piquillos

Piquillo peppers are native to Northern Spain and have a long, pointed shape resembling a "little beak," hence, the name. The peppers are mild and sweet in flavor and are most commonly available roasted, peeled, and preserved. They can be found online or in specialty stores. Mini sweet peppers are a suitable substitute.

---

8 ounces whipped cream cheese

1 tablespoon sherry vinegar

1 tablespoon extra-virgin olive oil

2 stalks celery, finely chopped

1 shallot, minced

2 tablespoons finely chopped fresh parsley

Pinch of red pepper flakes

1 cup lump crabmeat

8 *piquillo* peppers, stemmed and seeded

YIELD 8 PIQUILLOS

In a medium bowl, mix together the cream cheese, vinegar, oil, celery, shallot, parsley, and red pepper flakes. Using a rubber spatula, gently stir in the crabmeat until well combined. Using a spoon, fill the cavities of the *piquillo* peppers with the crab filling. Seal the top of each pepper with a toothpick and serve at room temperature.

Toothpicks & Skewers

Pintxos (Basque): Small bites, often pierced with toothpicks or skewers, meant to be eaten in one or two mouthfuls. *Pintxo* translates to "spike" or "thorn."

Banderillas: Skewered appetizers, common in Northern Spain, featuring pickled vegetables, fish, or olives and named for the decorated darts used in bullfighting.

Palillo: The Spanish word for "toothpick," also used to refer to a *pintxo*.

QUICK BITE IDEAS

- Olives, quail eggs, wax peppers, tuna, pickles, artichokes, onions
- Gherkins, olives, cocktail onions, bell peppers, *guindilla* (sweet pickled chile peppers)
- Black olives, green olives, Manchego cheese, feta cheese, cherry tomatoes, grilled hot peppers, cubed smoked ham
- Green apple, Brie, warm honey
- Cornichons, anchovy-stuffed olives
- Pickled carrots, pickled beets (cubed), roasted bell pepper, green olives
- Anchovies, pickled *guindilla* peppers, olives ("Gilda")
- Cheese, fish, eggs, sun-dried tomatoes, grilled meats, quail eggs
- Grilled figs, prosciutto
- Chorizo, *guindilla* pepper, young Manchego cheese

ROLLITOS DE BERENJA

Eggplant Rolls

This recipe is a Spanish take on the Italian *involtini*. Eggplant is thinly sliced and wrapped around a filling of soft cheese, ham, and fresh herbs. Choose a creamy cheese that melts well such as a young Mahón, a *tetilla*, or a young *ibérico*, which is similar to Jack cheese in its flavor, creaminess, and excellent melting capabilities.

2 large eggplants, thinly sliced lengthwise

2 tablespoons olive oil, plus 2 tablespoons for sautéing

Kosher salt and freshly ground pepper

2 cloves garlic, minced

5 ounces *jamón serrano*, chopped

5 ounces shredded melting cheese, such as Monterey Jack

1 tablespoon each finely chopped rosemary, thyme, and oregano

3 tablespoons honey

3 tablespoons Pedro Ximénez sherry vinegar or balsamic vinegar

YIELD 4 TO 6 SERVINGS

Brush the eggplant slices with 2 tablespoons of the oil and season with salt and pepper to taste. Coat a large sauté pan or grill with the remaining 2 tablespoons oil and warm over medium-high heat. Cook the eggplant until tender and golden brown in color, 2 to 3 minutes per side. Remove the eggplant from the pan and set aside to cool.

Meanwhile, in a small bowl, stir together the garlic, ham, cheese, and herbs (reserving 1 tablespoon for garnish) and season to taste with salt and pepper.

In a separate bowl, whisk together the honey and vinegar.

Preheat the oven to 350°F.

Spread 1 to 2 tablespoons of the filling onto each piece of eggplant. Roll each slice of eggplant and secure with a toothpick. Place in a lightly oiled baking dish. Brush the tops with the honey-balsamic mixture and roast for 10 to 15 minutes until the cheese has melted. Transfer to a serving platter and garnish with the reserved herbs.

Serve immediately.

CARNE AL ROMERO, PIQUILLO, Y CALÇOTS CON ROMESCO

Rosemary-Speared Beef with Piquillo, Grilled Scallions, and Romesco

This *pintxo* is inspired by the springtime Catalan festival *Calçotada*, which celebrates the arrival of a unique variety of scallions called *calçots*. The *calçots*, which are a larger version of the scallions used here, are grilled and served with grilled meats and romesco sauce.

---

2 tablespoons olive oil, plus more for the scallions

1½ teaspoons kosher salt, plus more for the scallions

½ teaspoon freshly ground pepper, plus more for the scallions

¼ teaspoon red pepper flakes

1 pound sirloin beef, cut into 1-inch cubes

2 tablespoons chopped fresh rosemary leaves, plus 16 whole sprigs fresh rosemary

1 bunch scallions, cleaned and trimmed

1 baguette, sliced and toasted

2 cups Salsa Romesco (page 117)

4 roasted and preserved *piquillo* peppers, quartered

YIELD 16 PINTXOS

In a large bowl, whisk together the oil, salt, black pepper, and red pepper flakes. Add the beef and stir to coat well. Cover and refrigerate for 2 hours, or overnight.

Preheat a grill to medium-high heat.

Sear the beef on the grill over medium-high heat until caramelized and golden, 4 to 5 minutes, turning occasionally. Using tongs, remove the meat from the grill and set aside.

On a plate, toss the whole scallions with oil, salt, and black pepper. Place on the grill and char, 10 to 15 minutes. The scallions will appear blackened on the outside but will be sweet and softened inside.

To assemble your skewers, brush the baguette slices with the salsa romesco and layer with the peppers, beef, and scallions. Skewer with a rosemary sprig and set on a platter to serve.

DÁTILES RELLENOS DE CHORIZO Y QUESO DE CABRA Y ENVUELTOS EN JAMÓN

Dates Stuffed with Chorizo and Goat Cheese Wrapped in Ham

Dates are more common in southern Spain, such as Andalusia. This classic tapa is the perfect combination of salty and sweet. Blue cheese makes an excellent substitute for the goat cheese, if desired.

1½ tablespoons chopped cured chorizo

2 teaspoons creamy goat cheese

½ teaspoon honey

8 Medjool dates, sliced lengthwise and pitted

4 slices *jamón serrano*, halved lengthwise

YIELD 8 STUFFED DATES

Preheat the oven to 400°F. Line a baking sheet with parchment paper.

In a small bowl, mix together the chorizo, goat cheese, and honey. Using a small spoon, fill the cavity of each date and wrap with a strip of *jamón*. Place the dates on the prepared baking sheet and bake for 10 to 15 minutes until caramelized, turning, if necessary.

Skewer with a toothpick and serve warm.

PINCHOS MORUNOS CON MOJO VERDE

Moorish Skewers with Green Mojo Sauce

These pork skewers showcase the Moorish influence on Spanish cuisine. The herbaceous sauce originated in the Canary Islands and is traditionally made using a mortar and pestle. Like chimichurri and *salsa verde*, it is loaded with fresh garlic and olive oil. The *mojo verde* serves as both marinade and dipping sauce in this dish.

If using bamboo skewers, be sure to soak them in water for at least thirty minutes before using to prevent them from burning.

½ bunch fresh flat-leaf parsley

½ bunch fresh cilantro

4 cloves garlic

½ cup olive oil

3 tablespoons sherry vinegar

2 teaspoons ground cumin

1 teaspoon kosher salt

¼ cup white wine

1 pound pork loin, sliced into 2-inch-wide pieces

YIELD 4 TO 6 SKEWERS

In the bowl of a food processor fitted with a metal blade, combine the parsley, cilantro, and garlic. Pulse until finely chopped. Add the oil, vinegar, cumin, and salt. Pulse to combine, then set aside half for serving.

Transfer the remaining sauce to a baking dish and add the wine to thin the sauce. Mix well. Thoroughly coat each piece of pork with the marinade, cover the dish, and refrigerate for at least 4 hours, or up to overnight.

Preheat the grill to medium-high heat or preheat the broiler to high.

Thread the pork pieces onto skewers, leaving a bit of space between each piece. Grill for 10 minutes per side. If using a broiler, place it on a rack several inches below the heating element for 8 to 10 minutes, or until the temperature registers 145°F on a meat thermometer. Serve with the reserved *mojo verde* sauce for dipping.

LANGOSTINO CON HUEVO COCIDO EN RODAJAS Y SALSA REMOULADE DE ALCAPARRAS SOBRE CROSTINI

Poached Prawn Speared with Hard-Boiled Egg and Asparagus on Crostini

This elegant springtime tapa features large, poached prawns and asparagus. The acidic and creamy aioli adds an extra flavor boost. Each component can be prepared in advance and assembled just before serving. Enjoy with Cava or sparkling sangria.

1 cup dry white wine

12 large prawns, peeled and deveined

4 sprigs fresh tarragon

Kosher salt

12 asparagus spears, tips trimmed into 2-inch pieces

½ cup mayonnaise

2 tablespoons white balsamic vinegar

1 shallot, minced

1 teaspoon capers

Freshly ground pepper

½ teaspoon finely chopped fresh tarragon, plus more for garnish

3 or 4 slices brioche, quartered and toasted

3 hard-boiled eggs, quartered

Extra-virgin olive oil for garnish

YIELD 12 TAPAS

Warm the wine and 1 cup of water in a shallow saucepan over medium-low heat. Add the prawns, tarragon sprigs, and a pinch of salt and gently poach until the prawns are opaque and pale pink in color, 8 to 10 minutes. Using a slotted spoon, transfer the prawns to a plate. Set aside to cool. Reserve the poaching liquid.

Bring the reserved liquid to a simmer, then add a pinch of salt and the asparagus tips. Gently poach over medium-low heat for 3 minutes until bright green in color with a slight limpness when picked up with a fork. Transfer to a bowl of ice water and set aside.

In a small bowl, whisk together the mayonnaise, vinegar, shallot, capers, and salt and pepper to taste. Stir in the chopped tarragon. Set aside.

Spread a generous spoonful of the caper aioli on the toasted brioche. Using a colorful toothpick, skewer the quartered egg with a prawn and asparagus spear and anchor into the brioche.

Drizzle with oil and a sprinkle of chopped tarragon and serve.

If you're short on time, use already-poached prawns from the fishmonger. White vinegar or champagne vinegar may be substituted for white balsamic vinegar.

MONTADITOS Y BOCADILLOS

Little Sandwiches

Montaditos are open-faced sandwiches spread with a topping; the name comes from "*montar,*" which in Spanish means "to place on top." *Bocadillos* are little sandwiches made with baguettes or rolls that have been halved lengthwise and filled.

Both of these tapas are simple and delicious and are served in most cafés and bars. People love them—they are portable and can be eaten as a midday meal or a filling snack. *Bocadillos* typically comprise meat, tuna, cheese, chorizo, or even a little omelet tucked between the bread. Served warm or cold, sometimes the sandwich bread is moistened by rubbing a cut tomato on it or adding a drizzle of olive oil.

CEREZAS AGRIDULCES CON QUESO DE CABRA, MIEL, Y BALSÁMICAS

Sweet and Sour Cherries with Goat Cheese, Honey, and Balsamic

This recipe highlights the *picota* cherry, a variety grown in the Jerte Valley near the Portugal border. Known as the "red diamond of Spain," the *picota* is prized for its deep-red color and intense sweetness, which develops during its long ripening time. However, you can use any fresh cherries, as *picota* cherries can be hard to find.

The cherry compote is also delicious served with ice cream or with the olive oil and almond cake (see page 130).

1 baguette, cut into ½-inch slices

Extra-virgin olive oil for brushing

2 cups *picota* cherries, pitted and halved

3 tablespoons dried sour cherries, softened in ¼ cup warm water

2 tablespoons sugar

Pinch of kosher salt

Freshly ground pepper

8 ounces creamy goat cheese

2 tablespoons white balsamic vinegar

2 tablespoons honey

YIELD 4 TO 6 SERVINGS (24 TAPAS)

Preheat the oven to 350°F. Line a baking sheet with parchment paper.

Brush the baguette slices with oil and place them on the prepared baking sheet. Cook until crisp and golden, about 10 minutes.

In the meantime, make the compote by simmering the fresh and dried cherries, 1 cup of water (or just enough to cover), the sugar, salt, and pepper to taste in a small saucepan over medium-low heat until the cherries soften and a thick syrup develops, about 10 minutes. Set aside to cool.

In a small bowl, whisk together the goat cheese and vinegar.

To serve, spoon the goat cheese onto the toast and top with the cherries and their juices. Drizzle the honey over the top and serve immediately.

If fresh cherries aren't available, preserved Amarena cherries work well, are delicious, and require no cooking. Add them to the dried cherries after they are poached.

PISTO DE BERENJENA

Spanish-Style Caponata with Eggplant and Onion Pisto

This dish is also known as the classic Sicilian dish caponata. It is a result of the Spanish and Arab influence on Sicilian food. Eggplant, originally from India, was introduced by the Arabs. It became an aristocratic dish, served with fish such as cod and tuna. Although delicious with fish, it is most commonly served in taverns and tapas bars with toasted bread.

---

1 eggplant

2 tablespoons plus ½ teaspoon kosher salt

4 tablespoons olive oil

¼ teaspoon freshly ground pepper

½ red onion, diced

1 green bell pepper, diced

2 Roma tomatoes, diced

2 cloves garlic, minced

6 olives, pitted and chopped

2 tablespoons pine nuts, toasted

2 anchovies, chopped

2 tablespoons golden raisins

2 tablespoons chopped fresh parsley

1 teaspoon capers

¼ teaspoon dried oregano

3 teaspoons Pedro Ximénez balsamic vinegar

Toasted baguette slices for serving

YIELD 4 TO 6 SERVINGS

Cut the eggplant into 2-inch cubes and place on a paper towel–lined platter. Sprinkle with 2 tablespoons of the salt and set aside for 10 minutes. Rinse under cold water and pat dry.

In a large sauté pan or skillet over medium-high heat, cook the eggplant with 2 tablespoons oil, remaining ½ teaspoon salt, and pepper until soft and golden, about 5 minutes. Transfer to a large bowl to cool.

Add another 1 tablespoon of the oil to the pan and sauté the onion, bell pepper, tomatoes, and garlic over medium heat for 3 to 5 minutes. Transfer to the bowl with the eggplant. Stir in the olives, pine nuts, anchovies, golden raisins, parsley, capers, oregano, and vinegar. Gently mix to combine. Drizzle with the remaining 1 tablespoon oil and adjust the seasoning, if needed. Cover and set aside for at least 4 hours. The flavors are even better if allowed to sit, refrigerated, overnight.

Serve with toasted baguette slices.

Store in an airtight container in the refrigerator for up to 5 days.

QUESO CABRALES CON COMPOTA DE MANZANA Y PERA SOBRE TOSTADA DE NUECES

Cabrales Cheese with Apple and Pear Compote on Walnut Toasts

Cabrales cheese comes from Cabrales, the "place of goats," in the Asturian region of Spain. The blue cheese is made either entirely of cow's milk, or a mixture of cow, goat, and sheep's milk. It is intense in flavor and aroma, with a creamy texture, and is often paired with something sweet to balance its bold flavor. Enjoy with a glass of Asturian cider.

COMPOTE

1 pear, peeled, cored, and diced

1 apple, peeled, cored, and diced

¼ cup dried apricots, coarsely chopped

¼ cup dried cherries

¼ cup golden raisins

1 cinnamon stick

2 strips orange zest

2 tablespoons sugar

TOASTS

8 ounces Cabrales cheese

1 loaf walnut bread, sliced into bite-size pieces and toasted

YIELD 4 TO 6 SERVINGS; 2 CUPS COMPOTE

To make the compote: Combine the pear, apple, apricots, cherries, golden raisins, cinnamon stick, orange zest, sugar, and 1 cup of water in a saucepan over medium heat. Bring to a boil, reducing the heat immediately to a simmer, then cover. Continue to cook at a simmer for 20 to 30 minutes until the apples and pears are soft but still retain their shape. Set aside to cool. Remove the cinnamon stick and zest.

To assemble: Generously spread some cheese on each of the walnut toasts. Top with a spoonful of compote.

Leftover compote will keep, refrigerated, for up to 3 days.

Spanish Toast

While Spain's tapas tradition is widely celebrated, the country's deep appreciation for uncomplicated, rustic desserts is equally profound. A perfect example is the cherished combination of toasted bread (*tostas*) with fruit compote. In Spain, toasted bread is a versatile canvas, often serving as a foundation for savory toppings. However, as evening arrives, it is often transformed into a sweet delicacy: thick slices of crusty bread toasted to a golden perfection and crowned with homemade fruit preserves. Whether made from apples, quince, or seasonal berries, these compotes elevate simple toast into a refined yet accessible treat. This beloved tradition of "*pan y fruta*" exemplifies Spain's mastery of elevating everyday ingredients and reflects a philosophy of resourcefulness where yesterday's loaf becomes today's delicious dessert.

BOCADILLO DE LOMO CON MOJO PICÓN

Pimentón-Marinated Pork Loin Sandwich

The spicy paprika in this smoky and garlicky *mojo picón* sauce, gives the pork a red hue. The addition of the caramelized onions on a toasted roll makes for a satisfying lunch or a sandwich on the go. It can be served hot or cold.

4 tablespoons olive oil

1 clove garlic, minced

½ teaspoon red pepper flakes

½ teaspoon paprika *picante*

1 teaspoon sherry vinegar

2½ teaspoons kosher salt

1 pound boneless pork loin, sliced crosswise into 1-inch-wide slices

1 yellow onion, sliced

1 tablespoon finely chopped fresh thyme leaves

4 sourdough rolls or baguettes, halved and toasted

½ cup arugula tossed with 1 tablespoon olive oil and a pinch of kosher salt

YIELD 4 BOCADILLOS

In a large dish, whisk together 2 tablespoons of the oil, the garlic, red pepper flakes, paprika, vinegar, and ½ teaspoon of the salt. Add the pork. Cover and refrigerate for several hours, or overnight.

Warm the remaining 2 tablespoons oil over medium heat in a large sauté pan or skillet. Add the onion, remaining 2 teaspoons salt, and thyme. Continue to cook until the onion is soft and translucent, 5 to 7 minutes. Using a slotted spoon, transfer to a bowl to cool.

Using the same pan, cook the pork and its marinade over medium-high heat for 5 to 7 minutes until tender and juicy and slightly pink in color.

Brush the rolls with the marinade from the pan and top each with several slices of pork and some of the onion. Add arugula and serve.

BOCADILLO DE TAPENADE VERDE Y DE ATUN

Seared Ahi Tuna with Green Olive Tapenade and Allioli Bocadillo

Manzanilla olives are the green olives of Spain and the most common olives in the world. Originally from Seville, the manzanilla is medium in size, with a meaty flesh and a tangy, salty flavor; it is loaded with antioxidants and healthy fats. Commonly used for oils and for snacking, it's what gives tapenade its distinctive color and sharp flavor.

This recipe is traditionally made using a mortar and pestle, but a food processor yields a blended paste that still retains a bit of the texture. Tapenade is an excellent addition to any tapas platter and is delicious on crackers or toast and as a dip for pickled vegetables.

TAPENADE

1 cup pitted green manzanilla olives

¼ cup olive oil, plus more as needed

¼ cup fresh parsley

3 cloves garlic, peeled and coarsely chopped

4 anchovies, coarsely chopped

2 tablespoons capers

2 teaspoons fresh lemon juice, plus more as needed

Kosher salt and freshly ground pepper (optional)

TUNA

8 ounces ahi tuna fillet, about 1½ inches thick

Kosher salt and freshly ground pepper

1 tablespoon olive oil

4 tablespoons Allioli (page 122)

4 sourdough rolls, sliced lengthwise and toasted

1 cup arugula, tossed with 1 teaspoon olive oil and a pinch of kosher salt

YIELD 4 BOCADILLOS; 1½ CUPS TAPENADE

To make the tapenade: Place all the tapenade ingredients in the bowl of a food processor fitted with a metal blade. Pulse until the mixture forms a coarse paste. Add more oil, if a more spreadable paste is desired. If needed, season with salt, pepper, and more lemon juice. Set aside.

To make the tuna: Season the tuna well with salt and pepper.

Warm the oil in a sauté pan or skillet over medium-high heat. Add the tuna and sear for 1½ minutes until lightly brown. Using tongs, turn the tuna and cook on the other side for another minute. The interior of the tuna should be rare. Transfer to a cutting board and slice lengthwise into ¼-inch-wide strips.

To assemble the *bocadillos*: Spread 1 tablespoon of the allioli on the top half of each roll, followed by 1 tablespoon of the tapenade on the bottom half of each roll. Top with the sliced tuna and arugula greens. Serve immediately.

Store leftover tapenade in an airtight container in the refrigerator for up to 1 week.

FRITOS, EMPANADAS, Y CROQUETAS

Fried Snacks, Savory Pastries, and Croquettes

Fritos refers to any Spanish dish that has been fried, often in olive oil. The practice of frying fish and vegetables in olive oil dates to Roman times.

Empanadas and their mini version, *empanadillas*, originated in Galicia. *Empanar* in Spanish refers to foods baked in pastry. The empanada is thought to be a descendant of the Arabic samosa. Spanish colonists later introduced the empanada to Latin America.

Empanadas can be savory or sweet and consist of a filling wrapped in pastry dough. Every cook in every region of Spain has their own version of the empanada, although the most common fillings consist of meat, fish, or vegetables. Designed to be portable, empanadas make a perfect addition to a picnic.

Croquetas are tapas filled with a mixture of meat, fish, vegetables, and a variety of spices.

EMPANADA GALLEGA

Galician Empanada

The Galician empanada is distinguished by its shape and filling. Traditionally made as one large, round pie with crimped edges, this empanada is filled with tuna and a *sofrito* of vegetables; it is cooked whole and served in wedges. Alternatively, as we do here, the empanada can be cooked in individual round tartlet pans, perfectly sized for tapas.

PASTRY

2½ cups all-purpose flour

1 teaspoon kosher salt

1 cup cold unsalted butter, cut into small pieces

½ cup ice-cold water

SOFRITO

3 tablespoons olive oil

1 onion, diced

1 green bell pepper, seeded and diced

2 cloves garlic, minced

3 plum tomatoes, chopped

½ teaspoon kosher salt

½ teaspoon freshly ground pepper

One 5-ounce can tuna, packed in oil, drained, and flaked

¼ cup green olives, pitted and coarsely chopped

1 hard-boiled egg, sliced

2 tablespoons chopped fresh parsley

2 teaspoons smoked paprika

1 large egg

1 tablespoon cream

YIELD 4 EMPANADAS

To make the pastry: Combine the flour, salt, and butter in the bowl of a food processor fitted with a metal blade. Process the mixture for about 10 seconds, or until it resembles fine breadcrumbs. With the motor running, slowly drizzle in the water until the dough starts to come together, about 30 seconds. Turn the dough onto a board and shape it into two equal rounds. Wrap each in plastic and chill for at least 1 hour.

Preheat the oven to 400°F.

To make the *sofrito*: Warm the oil in a large sauté pan or skillet over medium-low heat and add the onion, bell pepper, and garlic. Cook for 3 to 5 minutes until translucent. Add the tomatoes and season with the salt and pepper. Continue to cook for 5 minutes until the tomatoes release their juices. Set aside to cool.

Once cool, in a large bowl, combine the sofrito with the tuna, olives, hard-boiled egg, parsley, and paprika. Stir gently to combine.

In a small bowl, whisk together the raw egg and cream.

Roll out the dough and cut out eight 3-inch rounds. Press four of the rounds into the bottom of four tartlet molds. Divide the vegetable and tuna mixture among the molds and top each with another round of dough. Seal the edges and, using a paring knife, make two small vents in the top of each empanada. Brush the empanadas with the egg wash. Place the tartlets on a baking sheet and bake for 30 minutes until golden brown.

Store wrapped or in an airtight container in the refrigerator for up to 3 days.

EMPANADILLAS DE CHAMPIÑONES, CEBOLLA, Y QUESO

Mushroom, Caramelized Onion, and Cheese Empanadillas

A handheld *empanadilla* is similar to a turnover. In this recipe, they are filled with mushrooms, onions, and cheese, but you can also create different flavor combinations.

---

1 tablespoon olive oil

2 shallots, thinly sliced

8 button mushrooms, wiped clean and thinly sliced

1 clove garlic, minced

1 teaspoon kosher salt

1 teaspoon freshly ground pepper

1 teaspoon finely chopped fresh oregano leaves

2 teaspoons grated Manchego cheese, plus 1 tablespoon

One package (16 ounces) frozen puff pastry sheets, thawed

2 large eggs, lightly beaten with 1 tablespoon water

YIELD 14 EMPANADILLAS

Preheat the oven to 400°F. Line a baking sheet with parchment paper.

In a large sauté pan or skillet set over medium heat, warm the oil and cook the shallots for 3 minutes until translucent. Add the mushrooms, garlic, salt, pepper, and oregano and continue to cook for 5 minutes until the mushrooms are soft and have released their juices. Set aside to cool. Mix in 2 teaspoons of the cheese.

Place each pastry sheet on a lightly floured surface, gently rolling the dough to create an even surface. Divide into 8 equal squares and place about 1 tablespoon of filling on one half of the triangle. Using a pastry brush, brush the edges with egg wash and fold in half, enclosing the filling and forming a triangle. Using the tines of a fork, crimp the edges to seal. Transfer to the prepared baking sheet and repeat with the remaining dough and filling. Sprinkle the tops with the remaining 1 tablespoon cheese.

Bake for 20 minutes until golden and crisp. The *empanadillas* will keep in an airtight container in the refrigerator for several days.

EMPANADAS DE PICADILLO DE CARNE CON TAPENADE VERDE

Beef Picadillo Empanada

Picadillo comes from the Spanish word *picar*, meaning "to mince." Picadillo was a common dish in Spain during Moorish rule. It consists of ground meat, such as beef or pork, and a *sofrito* of vegetables (onions, garlic, peppers, and tomatoes).

1 tablespoon olive oil

½ red onion, diced

2 cloves garlic, minced

8 ounces ground beef

1 teaspoon kosher salt

½ teaspoon freshly ground pepper

1 cup diced tomatoes

3 tablespoons chopped fresh parsley

1 tablespoon capers, drained

1 tablespoon smoked paprika

1½ teaspoons golden raisins

One package (16 ounces) frozen puff pastry sheets, thawed

2 large eggs, lightly beaten with 1 tablespoon water

YIELD 24 EMPANADAS

Preheat the oven to 400°F. Line a baking sheet with parchment paper.

In a large sauté pan or skillet set over medium heat, warm the oil and cook the onion, garlic, and beef for 5 to 7 minutes until the beef is no longer pink. Season with salt and pepper. Add the tomatoes, parsley, capers, paprika, and golden raisins and continue to cook over low heat for 3 to 5 minutes. Set aside to cool. Adjust the seasoning, if needed.

Place each pastry sheet on a lightly floured surface and roll out the pastry to ⅛-inch thickness. Using a 3½-inch round cookie cutter, cut 24 rounds from the pastry. Spoon 1 tablespoon of filling on half of each round. Brush the edges with egg wash and press together to seal, crimping the edges with the tines of a fork. Transfer to the prepared baking sheet.

Bake for 20 minutes until golden and crisp.

Store in an airtight container in the refrigerator for up to 3 days.

CALAMARES A LA ROMANA

Fried Calamari

These fried calamari are made using the Roman culinary style of coating the squid in a light batter and frying it. Squid are a great source of lean protein and are rich in several vitamins and minerals. Highly perishable, squid should be stored for no more than 1 day in the refrigerator before cooking. Calamari is best cooked quickly at a high temperature so the fish remains tender.

---

1 pound squid, tubes and tentacles

1 cup rice flour

2 tablespoons cornstarch

2 teaspoons dried oregano

2 teaspoons kosher salt

1 teaspoon red pepper flakes

2 cups neutral vegetable oil, plus more as needed

1 lemon, sliced into wedges

1 cup Allioli (page 122)

YIELD 4 SERVINGS

Place the squid in a colander and rinse well with cold water. Pat dry with paper towels. Slice the tubes into ½-inch rings. Leave the tentacles whole. Set aside to dry thoroughly.

In a shallow dish, whisk together the flour, cornstarch, oregano, salt, and red pepper flakes. Add the squid and toss, coating well.

In a large, high-sided sauté pan or skillet over medium-high heat, warm the oil to 350°F. Add the squid in batches. Cook until golden, about 2 minutes. Using a slotted spoon, transfer to paper towels to drain. Allow the oil to get up to temperature again before repeating with the remaining calamari. Sprinkle with salt and serve with lemon wedges and allioli.

Store in an airtight container in the refrigerator for up to 2 days.

CROQUETAS DE POLLO

Chicken Croquettes

Croquetas are crunchy on the outside, with a creamy interior. They are an excellent way to use up leftovers. Simply coat the ingredients in a béchamel sauce, roll in breadcrumbs, and fry.

---

4 tablespoons butter

½ onion, diced

⅔ cup all-purpose flour, plus 2 tablespoons

1½ cups whole milk or light cream

2 teaspoons kosher salt

1 teaspoon freshly ground pepper

½ teaspoon ground nutmeg

2½ cups roast chicken, shredded

Neutral oil for cooking

1 large egg, whisked

1 cup panko breadcrumbs

YIELD ABOUT 36 CROQUETAS

In a large saucepan, melt the butter over medium heat. Add the onion and cook for 15 minutes until translucent. Add ⅔ cup of the flour, stirring well, and cook for 1 minute. Add the milk, a little at a time, stirring constantly. Add the salt, pepper, and nutmeg and continue to cook for 2 minutes. Stir in the chicken and mix well.

Spread the mixture onto a baking sheet and place in the refrigerator to chill for several hours. This will make the croquettes easier to shape.

In a large pan with high sides, heat the oil over medium-high heat until it reaches 375°F on a candy thermometer.

In three separate bowls, place the remaining 2 tablespoons flour, the egg, and the panko.

Use an ice-cream scoop to form the croquettes and then shape them by hand into thick rectangles. Dredge the croquettes in the flour, dusting off any excess. Dip in the egg and then in the breadcrumbs. Transfer the croquettes to the hot oil, being careful not to overcrowd the pan, and cook until golden brown on all sides, 3 to 5 minutes. Remove from the pan with a slotted spoon and place on a paper towel–lined plate to cool. Serve warm with *jamón* slices, halved, folded on top.

Store in an airtight container in the refrigerator for up to 2 days.

LA BOMBA

La Bomba (the Bomb) is believed to have originated in a bar in Barcelona, inspired by the bombings that occurred during the Spanish Civil War (1936–1939). These delicious ball-shaped *croquetas* of mashed potatoes are filled with meat, then breaded and fried. Enjoy with a fiery *salsa brava.*

1 pound Yukon gold potatoes, peeled and halved

Neutral oil for cooking

8 ounces ground pork

½ onion, finely chopped

1 clove garlic, minced

2 teaspoons kosher salt

1 teaspoon freshly ground pepper

1 teaspoon sweet paprika

1 cup all-purpose flour

2 large eggs, lightly whisked

1 cup breadcrumbs

2 cups Salsa Brava (page 123)

YIELD 12 CROQUETAS

To make the potatoes, fill a medium saucepan with water, add a large pinch of salt, and bring to a boil over high heat. Add the potatoes and cook over medium-high heat until easily pierced with a knife, 15 to 20 minutes.

In the meantime, warm 1 tablespoon oil in a large sauté pan or skillet over medium heat and add the pork, onion, and garlic. Stir in 1 teaspoon of the salt and ½ teaspoon of the pepper. Cook until the pork has browned and the onion is translucent, 5 to 7 minutes. Stir in the paprika and remove from the heat.

Using a slotted spoon, transfer the potatoes from the saucepan to a large bowl. Add 1 tablespoon oil and the remaining salt and pepper. Mash the potatoes until no lumps are visible. Set aside. Once cool, form into 2-ounce rounds. Flatten with your hand and place a bit of filling in the center. Close the potatoes around the filling and set aside.

To fry the potatoes, warm a large sauté pan or skillet over medium-high heat. Pour in about 1 inch of oil and add the potato *bombas*, working in batches. Fry until golden on all sides, 3 to 5 minutes. Remove from the pan with a slotted spoon and place on a paper towel–lined plate. Continue with the remaining potatoes.

Serve warm with the salsa.

Store in an airtight container in the refrigerator for 3 to 4 days.

CROQUETAS DE PESCADO Y GUISANTES

Cod and Shrimp Cakes with Potatoes and Peas

Russet potatoes are the best choice for these *croquetas*, as they have a high starch content that helps the fish cakes keep their shape and yields a crispy crust when fried.

12 ounces russet potatoes, peeled and quartered

8 ounces boneless cod fillet

2 tablespoons fresh lemon juice

3 tablespoons olive oil, plus more as needed

Kosher salt and freshly ground pepper

4 ounces peeled and deveined jumbo shrimp, cut into 1-inch pieces

1 large egg, lightly whisked

1 cup panko breadcrumbs

1 shallot, minced

2 tablespoons chopped fresh parsley

2 tablespoons frozen peas

1 tablespoon chopped fresh chives

Lemon wedges for serving

YIELD TEN 2½-INCH CROQUETAS

Preheat the oven to 400°F.

Bring a medium pot filled with salted water to a boil over high heat. Add the potatoes and cook until easily pierced with a knife, about 10 minutes. Using a slotted spoon, transfer the potatoes to a large bowl. Mash until no lumps are visible. Set aside to cool.

Place the cod in a small baking dish lined with parchment paper. Drizzle with the lemon juice and 1 tablespoon of the oil and season with salt and pepper to taste. Roast until the fish is firm and opaque, about 10 minutes. Remove from the oven and cool. Flake the fish over the mashed potatoes. Add the jumbo shrimp, egg, panko, shallot, parsley, peas, chives, 1 teaspoon salt, and ½ teaspoon pepper. Using a rubber spatula, gently mix until combined. Form the mixture into 2½-inch rounds. Flatten the tops and set aside.

In a large sauté pan or skillet over high heat, warm the remaining 2 tablespoons oil. When hot, cook the *croquetas* in batches until golden and crisp, about 3 minutes per side, taking care not to overcrowd the pan. Repeat with the remaining fish cakes, adding additional oil, if needed.

Serve warm with lemon wedges.

Store in an airtight container in the refrigerator for up to 2 days.

PATATAS BRAVAS CON SALSA BRAVA

Crispy Potatoes

These iconic "brave potatoes" are a cornerstone of Spanish tapas culture, loved for their simple, yet incredibly satisfying combination of crispy fried potatoes and bold, slightly spicy "fierce" *salsa brava*. A staple in bars across Spain, this is a dish that proves the best flavors often come from the most straightforward preparations.

1 pound Russet potatoes, peeled and cut into 2-inch cubes

½ cup olive oil

2 cloves garlic, peeled and left whole

2 teaspoons coarse salt

1 teaspoon smoked paprika

2 cups Salsa Brava (page 123)

YIELD 4 SERVINGS

In a pot of salted water, boil the potatoes over high heat until easily pierced with a knife, 5 to 7 minutes. Drain and set aside in a large bowl.

In a large sauté pan or skillet over meadium heat, warm the oil to 350°F. Place the garlic in the oil to flavor it, being careful to remove the cloves with a slotted spoon before they begin browning, which would make them bitter.

Add the potatoes to the pan and cook over medium-high heat until the exterior is golden brown and crisp, 10 to 15 minutes. Using a slotted spoon, transfer the potatoes to a paper towel–lined plate to cool. Transfer to a bowl to serve and toss with the coarse salt and paprika.

Serve immediately with the salsa.

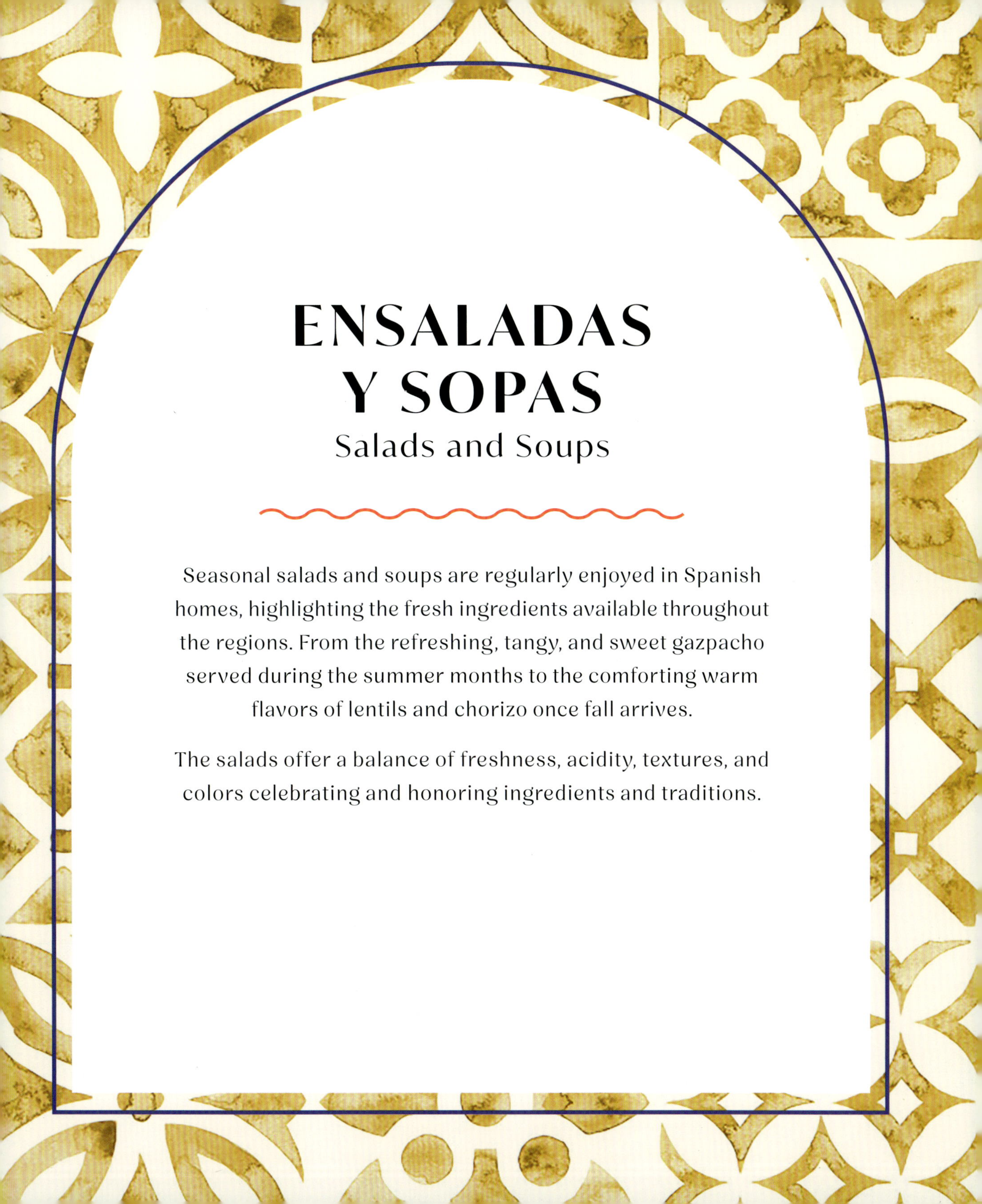

ENSALADAS Y SOPAS

Salads and Soups

Seasonal salads and soups are regularly enjoyed in Spanish homes, highlighting the fresh ingredients available throughout the regions. From the refreshing, tangy, and sweet gazpacho served during the summer months to the comforting warm flavors of lentils and chorizo once fall arrives.

The salads offer a balance of freshness, acidity, textures, and colors celebrating and honoring ingredients and traditions.

ENSALADA DE REMOLACHA CON MANZANAS VERDES Y ALMENDRAS

Beet Salad with Green Apples and Marcona Almonds

The beets give this salad an earthy sweetness that pairs nicely with the crisp, tart apples and creamy goat cheese. Any variety of beets will work well in this recipe, although it's nice to have an assortment of colors, if available.

The beets and the vinaigrette can be prepared and stored in the refrigerator up to 2 days in advance.

4 medium beets, cleaned and trimmed

¼ cup extra-virgin olive oil

2 teaspoons balsamic vinegar

Kosher salt and freshly ground pepper

2 cups arugula or mixed greens

2 shallots, thinly sliced

½ tart green apple, such as Granny Smith, julienned

¼ cup goat cheese, crumbled

¼ cup Marcona almonds, chopped

2 tablespoons chopped fresh parsley

YIELD 4 SERVINGS

Preheat the oven to 400°F.

Wrap each of the beets in aluminum foil and roast in the oven for about 40 minutes, or until they are easily pierced with a paring knife.

While the beets are cooking, whisk together the oil and vinegar in a medium bowl to make a vinaigrette. Season with salt and pepper to taste. Set aside.

Remove the beets from the oven and cool slightly. Using a paring knife, carefully remove the peel and slice crosswise into ¼-inch rounds. Set aside.

To assemble the salad, gently toss the greens and shallots with half the vinaigrette in a large bowl. Top with the beets and apple. Crumble the goat cheese over the top. Drizzle with the remaining vinaigrette. Garnish with the almonds and parsley. Serve immediately.

SALMÓN EN ESCABECHE

Salmon Escabeche

Escabeche is a traditional Spanish dish that originated in Persia. Fish or seafood is cooked or pickled in an acidic sauce. The tangy, bright flavors of the marinade perfectly balance the richness of the fish or seafood. Although easy to prepare, this dish makes an elegant tapa. Serve chilled or at room temperature.

1 pound wild-caught salmon fillet, cut crosswise into 1-inch-wide slices

1½ teaspoons kosher salt

2 teaspoons freshly ground pepper

1 shallot, thinly sliced

½ fennel bulb, trimmed and thinly sliced

4 sprigs fresh parsley, coarsely chopped

¼ cup extra-virgin olive oil

⅔ cup dry white wine, such as Albariño

4 cups mixed greens

2 tablespoons finely chopped fresh tarragon

YIELD 4 SERVINGS

In a glass dish, place the salmon slices and season well with salt and pepper. Add the shallot, fennel, and parsley.

In a small saucepan, heat the oil and wine over medium-high heat and boil for 1 minute. Immediately remove from the heat and pour the mixture over the salmon. Cover and set aside until cool. Transfer to the refrigerator and let the salmon marinate for at least 12 hours.

To serve, gently toss the greens with the vinaigrette from the marinade. Place the salmon pieces on top of the greens. Garnish with tarragon and serve.

PULPO A LA GALLEGA

Octopus Salad with Paprika Oil and Potatoes

Pulpo a la Gallega is the regional dish of Galicia, which is known for its abundance of delicious seafood, and this hearty dish has been prepared there for hundreds of years. The variation here is made more elegant by the addition of shallots and fennel, and the delicate flavors of the octopus and vegetables pair well with the crisp, buttery potatoes.

---

1 pound fingerling potatoes, halved lengthwise

5 tablespoons extra-virgin olive oil

1 teaspoon kosher salt, plus more for seasoning

1 teaspoon sweet paprika

1 pound octopus, cut into ½-inch rings, tentacles left whole

1 tablespoon sherry vinegar

½ teaspoon freshly ground pepper

4 cups mixed greens

½ fennel bulb, cored and thinly sliced

2 shallots, thinly sliced

1 tablespoon finely chopped fresh parsley

1 tablespoon minced fresh chives

YIELD 4 SERVINGS

Preheat the oven to 400°F.

Place the potatoes on a baking sheet and drizzle with 2 tablespoons of the oil. Season well with salt. Roast until the potatoes are golden and fork-tender, 30 to 40 minutes. Sprinkle with the paprika and toss well. Set aside to cool.

In a large sauté pan or skillet over high heat, warm 2 tablespoons of the oil and cook the octopus for 3 to 4 minutes until opaque in color. Using a slotted spoon, remove from the pan and drain on paper towels.

In a large bowl, whisk together the remaining 1 tablespoon oil and the vinegar until emulsified. Season with salt to taste and the pepper and add the greens to coat well.

In a separate bowl, mix together the potatoes, octopus, fennel, shallots, and parsley. Toss to combine.

To serve, place some greens on a plate and top with the potatoes and octopus mixture. Garnish with the chives.

GAZPACHO BLANCO CON PEPINO Y UVAS

White Gazpacho with Cucumber and Grapes

Gazpacho, which has been enjoyed since ancient Roman times, is a light, chilled soup made with fresh vegetables. This sweet and refreshing soup, white and green in color, is an elegant alternative to the more familiar tomato-based gazpacho.

2 cups stale bread cubes

⅓ cup blanched almonds, 2 teaspoons reserved

1 clove garlic

2 tablespoons chopped shallots, 1 teaspoon reserved

1 cucumber, peeled, seeded, and chopped, 2 teaspoons reserved

¾ cup green grapes

2 tablespoons extra-virgin olive oil

3½ teaspoons sherry vinegar

1 teaspoon kosher salt

YIELD 4 SERVINGS

Place the bread in a small bowl, cover with ½ cup of water, and set aside until the water is absorbed by the bread.

Place the almonds and garlic in a blender and blend until smooth. Add the remaining ingredients, plus 1 cup of water and the soaked bread. Blend until smooth. Adjust the seasoning as needed. Strain the mixture through a fine sieve.

Serve cold in tall glasses or glass bowls and garnish with the reserved almonds, shallots, and cucumber.

SOPA DE PATATAS CON FUGAS

Leek and Potato Soup

Leeks have long been an essential ingredient of Spanish home cooking, especially in the regions of Galicia and Asturias, where they are abundant. Potatoes were brought to this region from South America and thrive well in the cooler climate. This is a rustic and hearty soup and easy to prepare.

2 tablespoons olive oil

2 leeks, white parts only, sliced

3 teaspoons kosher salt

1½ teaspoons freshly ground pepper

1 pound russet potatoes, peeled and cubed

4 cups vegetable broth

4 sprigs fresh thyme, plus 2 teaspoons minced

1 teaspoon sweet paprika

1 tablespoon finely chopped fresh chives

Crusty bread for serving

YIELD 4 SERVINGS

In a large saucepan over medium heat, warm the oil and add the leeks. Season with 1 teaspoon of the salt and ½ teaspoon of the pepper and cook for 5 minutes until soft. Add the potatoes, broth, and thyme sprigs and bring to a boil. Add the remaining 2 teaspoons salt and 1 teaspoon pepper. Cover and simmer for 30 minutes until the potatoes are soft. Using an immersion blender, puree the soup until there are no visible lumps. Add the paprika and mix well.

Ladle into bowls and garnish with the 2 teaspoons minced thyme and the chives. Enjoy with crusty bread.

Store in an airtight container in the refrigerator for 3 to 4 days.

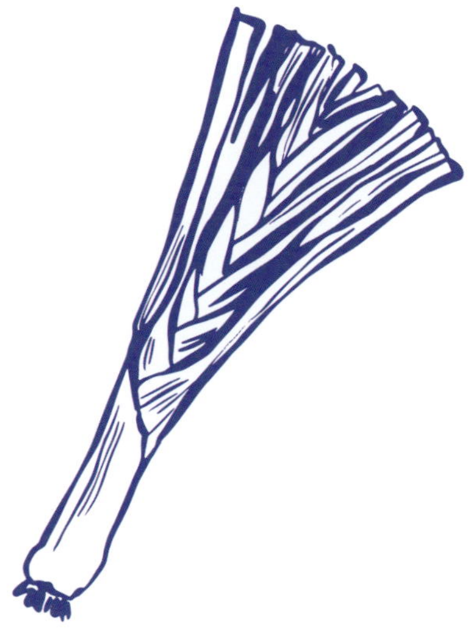

GAZPACHO ANDALUZ CON PAN RALLADO DE PIMENTÓN

Andalusian Gazpacho with Paprika Breadcrumbs

Gazpacho is a staple of Spanish cuisine and is a refreshing cold soup enjoyed almost daily during the summer months, especially in Andalusia. The smoked paprika breadcrumbs add a flavorful, crunchy finish.

1 cup stale bread cubes

1 red bell pepper, quartered and seeded

2 cloves garlic, chopped

2 large tomatoes, quartered and seeded

½ cup olive oil, plus 1 tablespoon

2 tablespoons sherry vinegar

1 cucumber, peeled, seeded, and cut into large pieces

1 teaspoon kosher salt

1 teaspoon smoked paprika

YIELD 4 SERVINGS

Add the bread to the blender and pulse until fine. Remove ¼ cup of the breadcrumbs and set aside.

Add the bell pepper, garlic, tomatoes, ½ cup of the oil, vinegar, cucumber, and salt to the blender and process until smooth. Transfer to a large bowl, cover, and refrigerate for at least 1 hour, up to overnight.

In the meantime, warm the remaining 1 tablespoon oil in a small sauté pan, over medium-low heat. Add the reserved breadcrumbs and the paprika, cooking until toasted and golden, 3 to 5 minutes. Set aside to cool.

To serve, ladle the gazpacho into individual bowls and garnish with the paprika crumbs.

For a thinner consistency, whisk 1 tablespoon of water at a time into the soup until the desired consistency is achieved.

Store in an airtight container in the refrigerator for 3 to 4 days.

SOPA DE LENTEJAS, ESPINACAS, Y CHORIZO CON CREMA DE AZAFRÁN

Lentil, Spinach, and Chorizo Soup with Saffron Cream

The chorizo not only gives this soup a fragrant and deep, smoky flavor, but it also adds a gorgeous color. This is a delicious cool-weather soup, and the lentils add loads of fiber and protein. Be sure to use French green or brown lentils, as these varieties retain their shape best after cooking.

1 tablespoon olive oil

1 carrot, peeled and diced

1 onion, diced

2 teaspoons kosher salt

1 cup French Puy lentils, rinsed well

One 14-ounce can plum tomatoes, chopped or cut with scissors in the can

4 to 6 cups vegetable broth, or water

1 cup sliced (1-inch pieces) chorizo

1½ cups spinach, cut into chiffonade

1 teaspoon smoked paprika

¼ teaspoon saffron threads, bloomed (see page 13)

½ cup plain yogurt

YIELD 4 TO 6 SERVINGS

In a large saucepan over medium heat, warm the oil and sauté the carrot and onion until the onion is translucent and soft, 3 to 5 minutes. Season with salt. Add the lentils, tomatoes and their juices, and 4 cups of the broth and continue to cook over medium heat until the lentils are tender, about 45 minutes. Add more broth, as needed. Stir in the chorizo, spinach, and paprika and continue cooking until the spinach is wilted, about 5 minutes.

In a small bowl, stir together the saffron and yogurt.

Ladle the warm soup into bowls and serve with a spoonful of saffron yogurt.

Store in an airtight container in the refrigerator for 3 to 4 days.

CAZUELAS

Casseroles

Cazuelas are sauced dishes cooked and served in the traditional earthenware pots of the same name. The Spanish make nearly everything in the durable, wide, and shallow *cazuelas*; they are ideal for cooking, as they can be used in the oven and on the stovetop, over low heat, and they retain heat well and allow for even and gentle cooking. They also make beautiful serving vessels. If you don't have a *cazuela*, a Dutch oven or a high-sided pan works well.

Typically, a more substantial dish, a *cazuela* requires utensils for eating. Spaniards regularly enjoy these dishes at home, and they are traditionally served with sherry or wine, or cider, if in Asturias.

VIEIRAS EN SALSA DE AZAFRÁN

Scallops in Saffron Sauce

Saffron has long been a highly desired and prized spice. It was originally introduced to Spain by the Moors, and the region of La Mancha now produces the majority of the world's saffron. This delicate spice yields a beautifully colored and richly flavored sauce and its earthiness perfectly complements the sweet and briny flavors of the scallops.

8 saffron threads

2 tablespoons olive oil

1 clove garlic, minced

12 scallops, rinsed and patted dry

½ teaspoon kosher salt

¼ teaspoon red pepper flakes

½ cup dry white wine

¼ cup heavy cream

1 tablespoon butter

2 tablespoons minced fresh chives

YIELD 12 SCALLOPS

To bring out the flavor and color of the saffron, crush it with a mortar and pestle and transfer to a bowl with 1 tablespoon hot water. Let soak for 1 minute.

In the meantime, in a large sauté pan or skillet, combine the oil and garlic and cook until lightly browned over medium heat to flavor the oil. Using a slotted spoon, remove the garlic. Add the scallops, season with salt and red pepper flakes, and cook for 4 to 5 minutes per side until firm and golden brown. Using tongs, transfer the scallops to a warmed serving bowl.

Add the wine to the pan and cook over medium heat until reduced by half, 3 to 5 minutes. Then add the cream and butter, along with the reserved saffron and its liquid, and cook until slightly reduced and small bubbles form, 1 to 2 minutes. Pour the sauce over the scallops and garnish with chives. Serve immediately.

CHAMPI RELLENOS CON ALBARINO

Stuffed Mushrooms

These are a delicious two-bite tapa. When cleaning mushrooms, be sure not to immerse them in water, as they will absorb the liquid. Instead, gently wipe with a damp cloth to remove any visible dirt. These can be prepared a day in advance and popped in the oven for an easy tapa.

---

8 cremini or white button mushrooms, cleaned and trimmed

Kosher salt and freshly ground pepper

3 tablespoons olive oil, plus more for drizzling

2 tablespoons finely chopped *jamón serrano*

1 shallot, minced

1 tablespoon minced garlic

¼ cup dry white wine

½ cup panko breadcrumbs

¼ cup grated aged Manchego cheese

1 tablespoon finely chopped fresh parsley

½ teaspoon paprika

YIELD 4 SERVINGS

Preheat the oven to 400°F.

Remove the stems from the mushroom caps and chop finely. Set aside. Using a teaspoon, gently clean out the inside of the mushroom caps. Place the caps in a baking dish lined with parchment paper, and season well with salt and pepper.

In a small sauté pan or skillet, warm 2 tablespoons of the oil over medium heat and cook the *jamón*, shallot, and garlic until shallot is translucent, 3 to 5 minutes. Season with 1 teaspoon of the salt and ½ teaspoon of the pepper. Add the mushroom stems and continue to cook for another 5 minutes until they have released their juices and are golden in color. Transfer to a large bowl and combine with the remaining ingredients, including the remaining 1 tablespoon oil.

Using a teaspoon, divide the filling among the mushroom caps, mounding it slightly. Drizzle with oil and roast until the mushrooms are golden brown and the filling is hot, for about 20 minutes.

Cool slightly before serving. Store in an airtight container in the refrigerator for 3 to 5 days.

BACALAO A LA VASCA CON PIPERRADA

Basque-Style Cod with Piperade Sauce

Piperrada (piperade) is a traditional dish of the Basque region, which straddles the border of Spain and France. It is said that the colors of the dish represent the Basque flag.

The meaning of *piper* in Basque is "pepper," the main ingredient in this dish, which also includes onions, tomatoes, garlic, and *piment d'Espelette*. The Espelette pepper, which is native to the region, adds a sweet, smoky, and fruity flavor to the dish. If you are not able to source the spice, substitute Spanish paprika or ⅛ teaspoon cayenne pepper.

The peppers are simmered over low heat to bring out their sweetness. The cod is braised in the peppers and its sauce, yielding a delicate and flavorful finish. The *piperrada* can also be served on its own with crusty bread, or as an accompaniment to other fish or chicken.

¼ cup olive oil

1 onion, thinly sliced

2 green bell peppers, thinly sliced

4 cloves garlic, thinly sliced

Kosher salt and freshly ground pepper

½ cup white wine, fish stock, or water

2 teaspoons *piment d'Espelette*

3 tablespoons tomato paste

1 tablespoon sweet paprika

1-pound fresh cod filet, 2-inches thick

2 tablespoons chopped fresh parsley

YIELD 4 SERVINGS

In a large sauté pan or skillet, warm the oil over medium-low heat. Add the onion, bell peppers, and garlic and season with 1 teaspoon salt and pepper to taste. Cook until the vegetables are soft, about 15 minutes. Add the wine, *piment d'Espelette*, and the tomato paste. Cook over medium heat for another 3 to 5 minutes. Add the paprika and stir to combine.

Season the cod with salt and pepper and gently place it in the pan, immersing it in the peppers and liquid. Cook over medium-low heat for 8 to 10 minutes until the fish is opaque and begins to flake.

Using a fish spatula, carefully remove the cod from the pan and divide it among four small bowls. Spoon the pepper mixture over the top. Garnish with parsley and serve immediately.

ALMEJAS CON CHORIZO

Clams with Chorizo

Dried, cured chorizo, which resembles salami, is commonly used in Spain. It is typically seasoned with lots of paprika, cured and dried for several months, and can be served as is, or cooked. This recipe calls for a small variety of clams called littleneck. Be sure to choose clams with shells that are tightly closed and discard any clams with broken or cracked shells.

4 pounds littleneck clams
1 tablespoon olive oil
⅔ cup chopped cured chorizo
2 shallots, thinly sliced
3 tablespoons minced garlic
1 teaspoon kosher salt
½ teaspoon freshly ground pepper
1 teaspoon smoked paprika
⅔ cup dry white wine
3 tablespoons unsalted butter
¼ cup chopped fresh parsley
¼ cup fresh lemon juice
Crusty bread for serving

YIELD 4 SERVINGS

Place the clams in a large bowl filled with cold water and swirl well to remove any sand or grit. Drain and cover again with cold water, and let sit for 20 minutes.

In a large sauté pan or skillet with a lid, warm the oil over medium heat and add the chorizo. Cook for 1 minute. Add the shallots and garlic and cook for another minute. Season with the salt, pepper, and paprika.

Drain the clams and add to the pan, along with the wine and butter. Cover the pan and simmer over medium-low heat for 5 minutes until the clams have opened. Discard any unopened clams. Stir in the parsley and lemon juice.

Serve immediately with crusty bread.

GAMBAS AL AJILLO

Spanish Garlic Prawns

These rich, delicious prawns are sautéed in lots of garlic and olive oil. Serve sizzling-hot in a shallow *cazuela* with plenty of crusty bread to soak up the juices. A squeeze of lemon at the end of cooking balances the richness of the oil and garlic.

2 tablespoons olive oil

4 cloves garlic, thinly sliced

½ cup white wine

Salt and freshly ground pepper

1 teaspoon smoked paprika

1½ pounds medium prawns, shelled and deveined

Juice of ½ lemon

1 teaspoon chopped fresh parsley

YIELD 4 TO 6 SERVINGS

In a medium sauté pan or skillet over medium heat, warm the oil and add the garlic, cooking for 1 to 2 minutes until lightly browned. Add the wine, salt and pepper to taste, and paprika and simmer until the liquid has reduced by half, about 2 minutes. Add the prawns and cook until the prawns begin to turn pink, 2 to 3 minutes. Using a non-slotted spoon, transfer to a bowl for serving.

Drizzle with lemon juice, sprinkle with the parsley, and serve immediately.

GUISO DE GARBANZOS Y ESPINACAS

Chickpea and Spinach Stew

Chickpeas, or garbanzo beans, have been a favorite food in Spain since their introduction by the Phoenicians in 800 BCE, and this hearty chickpea and spinach stew is a testament to their enduring appeal. Simple, yet deeply satisfying, it's a comforting dish and a flavorful glimpse into Spain's rich culinary history.

---

1 tablespoon olive oil

1 onion, chopped

1 clove garlic, finely chopped

1 carrot, chopped

2 teaspoons kosher salt, plus more as needed

1 teaspoon freshly ground pepper, plus more as needed

1 bay leaf

One 14-ounce can garbanzo beans, drained and rinsed

2 teaspoons sweet paprika, plus more as needed

3 tablespoons tomato paste

4 cups chicken broth

4 cups fresh spinach, rinsed and coarsely chopped

Crusty bread for serving

YIELD 4 SERVINGS

In a large saucepan, warm the oil over medium heat and add the onion, garlic, and carrot. Season with the salt and pepper. Add the bay leaf. Sauté until soft and translucent, 5 to 7 minutes. Add the garbanzo beans, paprika, tomato paste, and broth and cook over medium-low heat until the beans are tender and beginning to fall apart, 20 to 25 minutes. Remove the bay leaf and add the spinach and continue to cook for another 10 minutes until wilted. Season to taste with salt, pepper, and paprika.

Serve immediately with crusty bread.

Store in an airtight container in the refrigerator for 3 to 4 days.

ALBÓNDIGAS

Meatballs

Here's one meatball recipe that can be paired with two unique sauces and preparations.

The *albóndigas* with saffron-tomato sauce are baked, which allows the meatballs to keep their round shape. The *albóndigas* with almonds are simmered in the sauce, resulting in a tender and flavorful meatball. An ice-cream scoop is ideal for portioning the meatballs and allows for even cooking times and portions.

1 pound ground pork

1 pound ground beef

1 large egg

2 tablespoons tomato paste

1 tablespoon olive oil

¼ cup Rioja wine

2 teaspoons sherry vinegar

2 teaspoons kosher salt

Freshly ground pepper

2 teaspoons sweet paprika

1 slice white bread, torn into small pieces

½ yellow onion, peeled and quartered

2 cloves garlic, finely chopped

Handful of fresh parsley, coarsely chopped

YIELD 24 MEATBALLS

In a large bowl, combine the ground pork, ground beef, egg, tomato paste, oil, wine, vinegar, salt, pepper, paprika, and bread.

In the bowl of a food processor fitted with the metal blade, combine the onion, garlic, and parsley and process just until combined. Add the mixture to the pork and beef and gently mix by hand until just blended.

Using a large ice-cream scoop or ¼-cup measure, portion the meatballs and place them on the prepared sheet pan about 1 inch apart. Drizzle with oil and bake until golden brown and the internal temperature registers 160°F on a meat thermometer, 15 to 20 minutes.

The onions are chopped in a food processor, creating a slurry with the juices, which adds more moisture to your meatballs. A similar result can be achieved by grating the onions.

The Secret to Good Meatballs

In Spain, meatballs are known as *albóndigas*. The word *albóndiga* is derived from the Arabic word *albunduq*, which translates to "little round thing." *Albóndigas* most likely originated in Persia and were known as *kofta*. They were made with finely minced meat, spices, and rice or bulgur wheat, which helped bind the *kofta*. This practice of combining meat with spices was introduced to Spain during the Moorish occupation. Over time, *albóndigas* have become a staple of Spanish home cooking and tapas bars, with different regions creating their own versions of the meatballs, using regional ingredients and techniques. Traditional *albóndigas* from southern Spain are made with an almond *picada*, in which the nuts are finely ground and added to herbs and aromatics to lend flavor, color, and texture to the dish. In regions near the Mediterranean, the meatballs are made with minced fish, and in central Spain, they are simmered in an earthy tomato sauce.

ALBÓNDIGAS PICADA DE ALMENDRAS

Meatballs with Chopped Almonds

Many Spanish recipes of Arabic origin contain nuts, such as almonds. A *picada,* which is a mixture of garlic, parsley, and nuts, is ground into a fine paste and stirred into a dish toward the end of cooking, lending color, earthiness, and texture. Often used in *cazuela* dishes, *picar* means "to chop," although the *picada* is traditionally made with a mortar and pestle to release the oils of the nuts. The *picada* can also be made by pulsing the nuts in a food processor until just combined, as in this recipe.

¼ cup blanched raw almonds

1 slice white bread

2 cloves garlic, minced

2 tablespoons olive oil

3 tablespoons finely chopped fresh parsley, plus more for garnish

1 cup chicken broth

1 cup dry white wine

1 teaspoon kosher salt

1 pound ground pork, veal, or beef

½ cup breadcrumbs

1 large egg

1 teaspoon kosher salt

½ teaspoon freshly ground pepper

2 teaspoons sherry vinegar

YIELD 2 CUPS SAUCE

In the bowl of a food processor, pulse the almonds until finely ground, 15 to 20 seconds. Add the bread and garlic and pulse for another 10 seconds.

In a small sauté pan or skillet over medium heat, warm the oil and add the almond mixture. Toast until golden brown, 3 to 5 minutes. Transfer to a small bowl and stir in the parsley. Set aside.

In a large bowl, combine the ground pork, veal, or beef with the breadcrumbs, egg, salt, and pepper. Mix with your hands until just combined. Form the mixture into 1-inch (walnut-size) meatballs.

In a large sauté pan or skillet over medium heat, warm the broth and wine. Add salt, to taste, reduce the heat to low, and add the meatballs. Cover and simmer until the internal temperature of the meatballs registers 160°F on a meat thermometer, 15 to 20 minutes. Stir in the *picada* and continue to cook, uncovered, for another 20 to 30 minutes until the sauce is thick and the meatballs are tender.

Transfer the meatballs and sauce to a serving dish or plater. Drizzle with sherry vinegar and garnish with parsley.

Store in an airtight container in the refrigerator for 3 to 4 days.

ALBÓNDIGAS CON SALSA DE TOMATE AL AZAFRÁN

Meatballs with Tomato Sauce and Saffron

This sauce takes advantage of the abundance of juicy and flavorful summer tomatoes. If you do need to use canned, a 28-ounce can of whole plum tomatoes can be substituted.

The addition of the saffron to the recipe yields a rich and earthy sauce. The saffron needs to be steeped in a warm liquid, such as water, broth, or wine, before adding it to the dish. This critical step allows the flavor and color of the saffron to release.

Perfect as a single tapa or a dish for a larger gathering, the meatballs also make a delicious and hearty *bocadillo* when served on a baguette with Allioli (page 122) and arugula.

½ cup dry white wine

1 teaspoon saffron threads

2 tablespoons olive oil, plus more for drizzling

2 cloves garlic, peeled

8 to 12 Roma tomatoes, quartered

¼ teaspoon red pepper flakes

2 teaspoons salt

Freshly ground pepper

1 teaspoon sugar

1 recipe Albóndigas (page 99)

YIELD 3 CUPS SAUCE

Preheat the oven to 375°F. Line a sheet pan with parchment paper.

In a small saucepan over medium-low heat, warm the wine and add the saffron. Set aside, off the heat, for 10 minutes.

In a large saucepan, warm the oil over medium heat and add the garlic, tomatoes, red pepper flakes, salt and pepper to taste, and sugar. Add the wine and saffron and continue to simmer over medium-low heat until the sauce thickens and the flavors mellow, about 1 hour. Turn off heat and let sit.

Prepare the meatballs as instructed in the *Albóndigas Picada de Almendras* recipe (page 99). Using a large ice-cream scoop or ¼-cup measure, portion the meatballs and place them on the prepared sheet pan about 1 inch apart. Drizzle with oil and bake until golden brown and the internal temperature registers 160°F on a meat thermometer, 15 to 20 minutes.

Ladle the sauce into a bowl and place the meatballs on top to serve.

ARROZ NEGRO VALENCIANO CON PULPO Y ALLIOLI DE LIMÓN

Valencian Black Rice with Squid and Lemon Allioli

This rice, which gets its distinctive black color from squid ink, is a common dish served along the Mediterranean coast of Spain, where squid is abundant. The squid and the ink give the dish a rich, briny flavor. The addition of the squid rings and tentacles gives this dish a dramatic look.

8 ounces squid, cleaned and patted dry

4½ cups fish stock or water

Two ¼-ounce packs squid ink

3 tablespoons olive oil

½ yellow onion, diced

½ green bell pepper, diced

2 cloves garlic, minced

1½ cups Valencia rice

2 teaspoons kosher salt

1 teaspoon freshly ground pepper

2 tablespoons chopped fresh parsley

1 lemon, sliced into wedges

Allioli (page 122)

YIELD 4 SERVINGS

Using a chef's knife, slice the squid pieces into rings, leaving the tentacles whole.

In a large saucepan, warm the stock and the squid ink over low heat. Set aside.

In another large saucepan, warm 2 tablespoons of the oil over medium heat. Add the squid pieces and cook until golden, about 2 minutes. Take care not to overcook the squid, as it can become tough. Using a slotted spoon, transfer it to a bowl and set aside.

And the remaining 1 tablespoon oil to the pan and sauté the onion, bell pepper, and garlic over medium-low heat for 5 to 7 minutes. Add the rice and cook until opaque, 3 to 5 minutes. Season with salt and pepper, then add the warm stock, 1 cup at a time, over medium-high heat. Once the stock has been absorbed into the rice, add another cup, stirring frequently, until the rice is al dente, 15 to 20 minutes.

Serve immediately. Garnish with parsley, lemon wedges, and allioli to taste.

Squid ink can be found online or at a specialty food store. Also, if you don't have Valencia rice, use another short-grain rice, such as Bomba or arborio.

ARROZ CON POLLO CON PICADA

Chicken with Rice and Picada

Unlike paella, which is a "dry" rice dish, *arroz con pollo* is typically cooked in a *cazuela* and has a moist, almost soupy consistency. Simple, yet satisfying, cazuela rice dishes are common family meals. This one is finished with an almond *picada* that lends a nutty, earthy flavor. The rice is cooked *al punto*, or "with just a bite."

The Catalan tradition of using almond *picada* in sauces dates back to the thirteenth century.

ARROZ CON POLLO

2 to 3 tablespoons olive oil

1 onion, finely chopped

1 stalk celery, finely chopped

1 carrot, peeled and finely chopped

1 teaspoon kosher salt, plus more as needed

Freshly ground pepper

3 or 4 boneless chicken thighs, cut into 1-inch pieces

4½ cups chicken broth

1½ cups short-grain rice

PICADA

2 cloves garlic, minced

¼ cup blanched almonds, toasted

Pinch of kosher salt

½ bunch fresh flat-leaf parsley, chopped

YIELD 4 SERVINGS

To make the chicken and rice: In a medium saucepan, pour in enough oil to coat the bottom of the pan. Warm the oil over medium heat and sauté the onion, celery, and carrot until soft and translucent, 5 to 7 minutes. Season with the salt and pepper to taste. Add the chicken and cook for 3 to 5 minutes. Add the broth and raise the heat to high. Add the rice and cook over medium-low for 8 to 10 minutes, stirring occasionally, until the rice is *al punto*, but still a bit soupy.

To make the *picada*: Using a mortar and pestle, crush the garlic with the almonds and salt until you have a smooth paste. Add the parsley and pound to mix well. Alternatively, a small food processor can be used. Stir the *picada* into the cooked rice dish, adding depth, texture, and color. Add salt and pepper to taste. Serve immediately.

Store in an airtight container in the refrigerator for 3 to 4 days.

PAELLA CLÁSICA

Classic Paella

Although paella is not strictly defined as a tapa, it is regularly served at tapas bars, often in small dishes such as *cazuelas*.

Paella was born in Valencia, and it is one of Spain's best-known and most cherished dishes. Originally cooked outside over an open fire and with rice as the central ingredient, paella's origins are humble—it was a dish consisting of food found in the fields and made as a filling meal for the workers.

When making paella, it is imperative to use a short- or medium-grain rice, such as Bomba or Valencia rice, which absorbs three times its volume in liquid and maintains its shape during cooking. Arborio rice is suitable as a substitute; however, use only 1 cup of rice per 2 cups of broth and be sure not to stir. The result will be sticky.

About Paella

The dish was originally called paella Valenciana, after the pan in which it was cooked (a *paellera*) and the area where the dish was born.

A key component of a successful paella is the proper development of the *socarrat*, the caramelized crust that forms at the bottom of the pan. To achieve the *socarrat*, which means "charred" or "scorched," cook the paella in a wide, shallow pan, don't overfill it, and refrain from scraping the bottom. Do not stir.

Choose a sweet (*dulce*) paprika (*pimentón*), the most common kind. *Pimentón* is delicate and burns easily, so add it at the very end of the *sofrito*.

Onions are not included because they add too much moisture.

Traditionally consisting of chicken, rabbit, snails, and fresh beans, paella ingredients now vary from region to region and include meat, seafood, and vegetables.

Rice was introduced to Spain by the Arabs in the eighth century and first planted around Valencia. The Spanish word for "rice," *arroz,* comes from the Arabic word for "lake," as the grain grows near the water. The finest Spanish rice is still grown in Valencia.

When using Bomba rice, allow for ⅓ cup uncooked rice per person. If using Valencia rice, allow ½ cup uncooked rice per person.

PAELLA VALENCIANA

Paella Valenciana is the original paella dish and was traditionally made with rabbit, chicken, and a few types of beans. The recipe here is a variation on the original paella and not only includes chicken, but also seafood and vegetables. The addition of the *salmorra* gives the broth a nice, deep flavor.

½ cup dried Nora peppers, stemmed and seeded

3 tablespoons olive oil

2 large tomatoes, seeded and chopped, plus 2 ripe medium tomatoes, seeded, then grated on a box grater

6 cups chicken broth

¼ teaspoon saffron threads, crushed

1 pound boneless chicken thighs, cut into 2-inch pieces

2 teaspoons kosher salt

2 bell peppers, seeded and sliced into strips

1 clove garlic, minced

1 teaspoon sweet paprika

2 cups Bomba rice

2 tablespoons chopped fresh parsley

YIELD 6 SERVINGS

To make the *salmorra*, place the Nora peppers in a small bowl of hot water to rehydrate. Once softened, chop well and add to a large saucepan with 1 tablespoon of the oil and the chopped tomatoes. Cook over medium-low heat until the sauce thickens and achieves the consistency of marmalade. Using a handheld immersion blender, puree until smooth. Add the chicken broth and bring to a simmer. Add the saffron.

In an 18-inch-wide paella pan, warm the remaining 2 tablespoons oil over medium heat and add the chicken. Season with salt. Cook until golden brown, 5 to 7 minutes, turning frequently. Add the bell peppers, grated tomatoes, garlic, and paprika and cook for another 5 minutes. Add the rice and stir well, then cook for 15 to 20 minutes, adding the broth mixture 1 cup at a time and allowing the liquid to be fully absorbed by the rice before each addition. Stir well. When the rice is al dente, reduce the heat to medium-low and top it with the mussels, prawns, clams, and peas. Continue to cook until the rice has developed a nice *socarrat* on the bottom and all the shells have opened, about 10 minutes more. Discard those that do not open. Garnish with parsley and serve from the pan.

Store in an airtight container in the refrigerator for 3 to 4 days.

PAELLA PRIMAVERA

Spring Paella

A vegetarian version of paella Valenciana. This dish celebrates spring with the abundance of fresh green vegetables and herbs. Feel free to substitute other seasonal vegetables to create this dish year-round.

3 tablespoons olive oil

2 leeks, cleaned, trimmed, and sliced into ½-inch wide rings

Kosher salt

1 pound asparagus spears, trimmed and cut into thirds

2 tablespoons minced fresh thyme leaves

2 cups Bomba rice

6 cups vegetable stock

1 cup drained and quartered marinated artichoke hearts

½ cup peas

¼ cup basil pesto

¼ cup snipped fresh chives

YIELD 6 SERVINGS

In an 18-inch-wide paella, warm the oil over medium heat and add the leeks. Season with salt and cook until soft and translucent, about 5 minutes. Add the asparagus and thyme and cook for another 5 minutes. Add the rice and stir well, cooking for 15 to 20 minutes. Add the broth 1 cup at a time, allowing the liquid to be fully absorbed by the rice before each addition. When the rice is al dente, reduce the heat to medium-low and top the rice with the artichoke hearts and peas. Continue to cook until the rice has developed a nice *socarrat* on the bottom, 5 to 10 minutes more. Stir in the basil pesto. Garnish with the chives and serve from the pan.

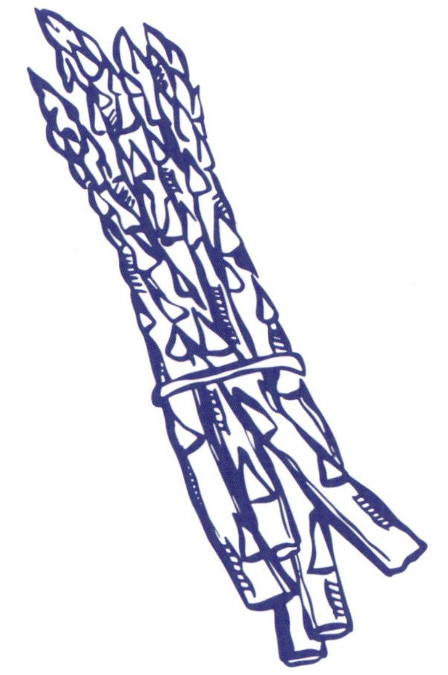

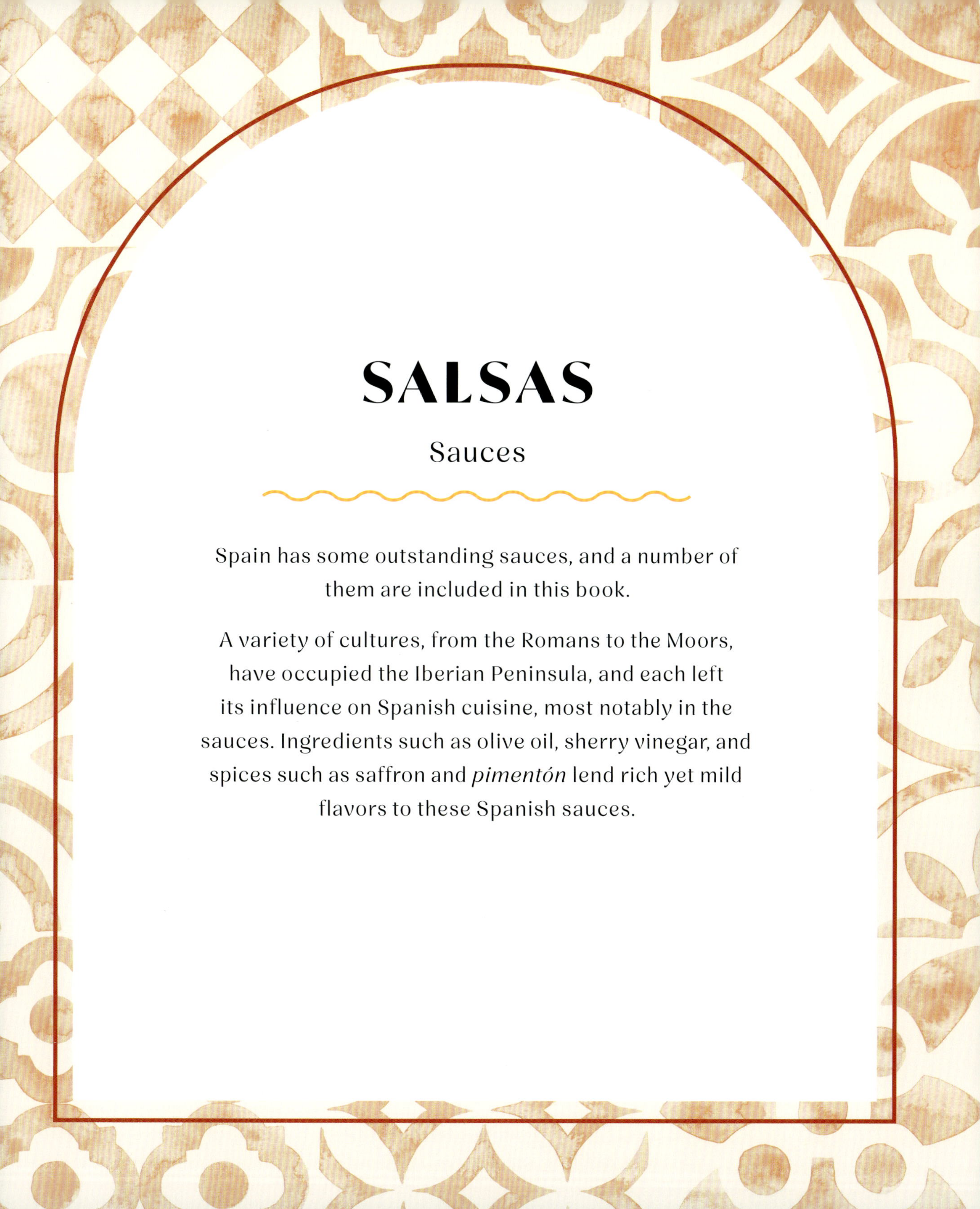

SALSAS

Sauces

Spain has some outstanding sauces, and a number of them are included in this book.

A variety of cultures, from the Romans to the Moors, have occupied the Iberian Peninsula, and each left its influence on Spanish cuisine, most notably in the sauces. Ingredients such as olive oil, sherry vinegar, and spices such as saffron and *pimentón* lend rich yet mild flavors to these Spanish sauces.

SALSA ROMESCO

Romesco is a classic smoky sauce from Catalonia in which the vegetables are blistered and the sauce is thickened by the addition of nuts and breadcrumbs. It is delicious with grilled meats and vegetables.

---

2 plum tomatoes

2 red bell peppers

1 clove garlic

2 tablespoons blanched almonds

2 tablespoons breadcrumbs

1 cup olive oil

2 tablespoons sherry vinegar

Kosher salt and freshly ground pepper

YIELD 1½ CUPS

Preheat the oven to 450°F.

Place the tomatoes and bell speppers on a baking sheet and roast until the skins have blistered and blackened, 20 to 25 minutes. Transfer to a bowl and cover with plastic wrap. Set aside. Once cool, remove the skins from the vegetables, reserving the juices.

In a food processor, combine the garlic and almonds and process until finely ground.

MOJO VERDE

Its bright-green color and fresh flavors make *mojo verde* a delightful accompaniment to a wide range of dishes, infusing them with its distinctive garlic and herb notes. Serve this versatile and herbaceous sauce with pork, chicken, fish, or potatoes. It also makes a delicious marinade.

½ bunch fresh flat-leaf parsley

½ bunch fresh cilantro

4 cloves garlic

½ cup extra-virgin olive oil

3 tablespoons sherry vinegar

2 teaspoons ground cumin

1 teaspoon kosher salt

¼ cup white wine (optional; for marinade)

YIELD 1½ CUPS

Place the herbs and garlic in the bowl of a food processor fitted with a metal blade. Pulse until the herbs are finely chopped.

In a medium bowl, combine the chopped herbs and garlic with the oil, vinegar, cumin, and salt.

To use as a marinade, stir in the wine. Store in an airtight container in the refrigerator for up to 5 days.

MOJO ROJO

This spicy and flavorful sauce originated in the Canary Islands and has African, Caribbean, and Portuguese influences. The *mojo rojo* is a classic red sauce traditionally made with a mortar and pestle with roasted peppers, garlic, vinegar, and spices. *Mojo picón* is a spicier variation of the red sauce, with red pepper flakes lending the heat. The word "*picón*" is derived from the verb "*picar*," which means "to sting." These sauces make delicious marinades for chicken, pork, or beef or dipping sauces for potatoes or grilled fish.

2 red bell peppers, roasted, seeded, and peeled (see page 117)

3 cloves garlic

2 teaspoons kosher salt

2 teaspoons smoked paprika

1½ teaspoons sherry wine vinegar

½ teaspoon ground cumin

YIELD 1 CUP

Combine all the ingredients in a blender and puree on high speed until smooth.

Store in an airtight container in the refrigerator for up to 3 days.

Mojo Picón Variation
Add ¼ teaspoon red pepper flakes before blending.

PIQUILLO CHUTNEY

Bright, tangy, and distinctly Spanish, this chutney is a vibrant addition to any tapas spread. Inspired by Spain's love for preserving peak-of-season produce, this versatile chutney is ideal spooned on grilled toasts, paired with creamy cheeses, or served alongside grilled meats and roasted vegetables. If you can't find *piquillo* peppers, use roasted red bell peppers.

2 tablespoons extra-virgin olive oil

2 red onions, peeled and thinly sliced

2 cloves garlic, peeled and left whole

1 teaspoon mustard seeds, crushed

1 teaspoon coriander seeds, crushed

6 whole cloves, crushed

½ teaspoon grated peeled fresh ginger

½ teaspoon ground turmeric

½ teaspoon red pepper flakes

2 preserved *piquillo* peppers, thinly sliced

¼ cup golden raisins, plumped in ½ cup boiling water

1 cup cider vinegar

1 cup light brown sugar

YIELD 2 CUPS

In a medium saucepan over medium heat, warm the oil and sauté the onions and garlic with the spices until soft, about 5 minutes. Add the *piquillo* peppers.

Stir in the golden raisins, vinegar, and brown sugar and continue to cook over medium-low heat until thickened, 30 to 40 minutes.

Use immediately or transfer to a tightly sealed jar to preserve. The chutney will keep for up to 6 months when stored in a cool place. Once opened, keep in the refrigerator and use within 1 month.

Coriander and mustard seeds are two of the oldest known spices. Native to the Mediterranean and Middle East, these seeds were used throughout ancient Greece and Rome to preserve meats and to make perfume. Today, the seeds are commonly used in pickling and chutneys to add a richer, spicy, and briny flavor and aroma. They also add texture. When using, crush the whole seeds gently with a mortar and pestle before adding to the pan. Toasting lightly in a dry sauté pan before using will enhance the flavor of the spices.

ALLIOLI

Originally from Catalonia and traditionally made in a mortar and pestle using only oil (*oli*) and garlic (*ajo*), this version of aioli includes egg yolks. Use the highest quality extra-virgin olive oil you can when making it. If you don't have a mortar and pestle, use a whisk or food processor (as with this recipe) to make the sauce.

---

2 cloves garlic

Kosher salt

2 egg yolks, at room temperature

1 cup extra-virgin olive oil

YIELD 1 CUP

Place the garlic on a cutting board and sprinkle with salt. Using a chef's knife, mince the garlic into a fine paste. Transfer the paste to a food processor and add the egg yolks and 2 tablespoons of the oil. Process for 1 minute. With the motor running, add the remaining oil in droplets until the mixture begins to emulsify. Continue adding the remaining oil in a slow, steady stream. Add more salt to taste. The allioli will keep in an airtight container in the refrigerator for up to 2 days.

Variation

Lemon: Add the zest of 1 lemon and 1 teaspoon fresh lemon juice at the end of processing.

Pimentón: Add 1 teaspoon finely chopped roasted *piquillo* peppers at the end of processing.

SALSA BRAVA

This Spanish "fierce" sauce has a spicy kick. Typically served with Patatas Bravas (page 73), it is equally delicious with grilled meats and fish. Note that paprika burns easily, so be sure to add it toward the end of cooking.

---

2 tablespoons olive oil

1 onion, coarsely chopped

3 cloves garlic, chopped

1 teaspoon kosher salt

1 tablespoon tomato paste

2 tablespoons all-purpose flour

1 cup vegetable broth or water

1 tablespoon sweet paprika

2 teaspoons smoked paprika

2 teaspoons sherry vinegar

YIELD 1 CUP

In a medium sauté pan or skillet, warm the oil over medium-high heat. Add the onion and garlic and sauté until soft and translucent, 5 to 7 minutes. Season with the salt. Reduce the heat to low, add the tomato paste, and stir for 1 minute. Add the flour, stirring and cooking for another 1 to 2 minutes. Whisk in the broth and raise the heat to medium-low. Continue to cook, stirring frequently, until the mixture has thickened, 8 to 10 minutes. Reduce the heat to low and add the paprikas, stirring well to combine. Stir in the vinegar. Set aside to cool. Using an immersion blender or a standard blender, puree the sauce until smooth. Serve immediately.

Store in an airtight container in the refrigerator for up to 5 days.

TAPAS DE POSTRE Y SANGRÍA

Sweets and Sangria

Spain's desserts are a celebration of its rich cultural diversity, traditions, and holidays. They are essential to Spanish cuisine, and each region and city has its own unique specialties. Many were created by the nuns in the convents to mark not only certain religious celebrations, but also to highlight the ingredients common to a particular region.

CHURROS CON CHOCOLATE

Churros

Churros are fried dough pastries eaten for breakfast or as a late-night snack along with a thick and rich chocolate dipping sauce; they were likely introduced to Spain by the Arabs. The name comes from the *Churra* breed of sheep in Castile, as the spiral shape of the pastries resembles the horns of the sheep.

During the sixteenth century, while exploring Mexico, the Spanish were introduced to a bitter drink called *xocolatl*, made from ground cacao beans and spices and enjoyed by the Aztecs. The cacao beans were brought back to Spain, where the drink was sweetened with sugar and vanilla. It was enjoyed mostly by the aristocracy, who kept it a secret from the rest of Europe for nearly a hundred years.

CHOCOLATE DIPPING SAUCE

1 cup dark semisweet chocolate, chopped

1 cup heavy cream

CHURROS

4 to 6 cups neutral oil

¼ cup extra-virgin olive oil

1 cup sugar plus 2 tablespoons

¼ teaspoon kosher salt

1 cup all-purpose flour

1 large egg

¼ cup ground cinnamon

YIELD 16 CHURROS

To make the chocolate dipping sauce: Place the chocolate in a large, heatproof bowl and set aside. In a small saucepan over medium-low heat, gently warm the cream until small bubbles form on the edges, 8 to 10 minutes. Do not boil. Pour the warm cream over the chocolate and whisk until combined and smooth.

To make the churros: Line a baking sheet with parchment paper.

Fill a large pan with high sides halfway with the oil and attach a candy thermometer. Heat the oil over high heat to 375°F.

Place 1 cup of water, the olive oil, 2 tablespoons of the sugar, and salt in a small saucepan and bring to a boil over medium-high heat. Remove from the heat and, using a wooden spoon, stir in the flour and continue to mix until the dough is smooth and begins to pull away from the sides of the pan. Set aside to cool. Transfer to the bowl of a stand mixer fitted with a paddle attachment. Add the egg and beat until combined.

Using a rubber spatula, scoop the dough into a pastry bag fitted with a star tip. Pipe 6-inch-long strips onto the prepared baking sheet. Once all the churros have been formed, carefully transfer, a few at a time, to the hot oil and fry until golden and crispy, 3 to 5 minutes. Using a large, slotted spoon, transfer to a paper towel–lined platter. Check the temperature of the oil before continuing with the remaining churros.

In a wide bowl, whisk together the remaining 1 cup sugar and cinnamon. Gently roll the churros in the cinnamon-sugar mixture and serve warm with the chocolate dipping sauce.

The churros will keep in an airtight container in the refrigerator for up to 2 days.

PERAS ESCALFADAS EN VINO TEMPRANILLO

Pears Poached in Tempranillo Wine

Tempranillo is a red wine grape from Northern Spain. The wine is deep red in color and has a smoky, spicy flavor. The beautiful color of the wine infuses the pears, resulting in an elegant-looking dessert.

2 cups Tempranillo wine

3 tablespoons granulated sugar

1 cinnamon stick

¼ teaspoon whole cloves

⅛ teaspoon whole black peppercorns

2 pears, halved and cored

½ cup heavy cream

1 tablespoon confectioners' sugar

YIELD 4 SERVINGS

In a medium saucepan, combine the wine, granulated sugar, and spices and bring to a boil over high heat. Reduce the heat to low and place the pears, cut-side down, in the poaching liquid. Simmer over low heat for 20 to 30 minutes until the fruit can be easily pierced with a knife. Using a slotted spoon, remove the pears from the poaching liquid and set aside. Reserving the liquid, continue to heat until the liquid has reduced by half and resembles a syrup, 20 to 25 minutes.

In a medium bowl, whip the cream with the confectioners' sugar until soft peaks form.

Place each pear half on a serving plate, add a spoonful of the whipped cream, and drizzle with the poaching syrup.

PASTEL DE ALMENDRAS Y ACEITE DE OLIVA CON AZAHAR, NARANJAS POCHADAS, Y NATA MONTADA

Almond and Orange-Blossom Olive-Oil Cake with Poached Oranges and Whipped Cream

This cake is incredibly moist and light and is perfumed by the orange blossom water and zest, which bring out the flavor of the olive oil. Olive oil is commonly used in baking throughout the Mediterranean. The oil yields a delicious, light cake. Use a high-quality, fruity, and mild Spanish olive oil so as not to overwhelm the delicate citrus flavors.

OLIVE-OIL CAKE

1½ cups granulated sugar

3 large eggs, at room temperature

Zest of 1 orange

¾ cup olive oil

3 teaspoons orange blossom water

2 teaspoons fresh orange juice

1¼ cups almond flour

1¼ cups all-purpose flour

1 tablespoon baking powder

½ teaspoon kosher salt

1 cup whole milk

CANDIED ORANGES

½ cup water

½ cup granulated sugar

1 navel orange, halved and sliced into 1-inch-wide half-moons

1 blood orange, halved and sliced into ide half-moons

WHIPPED CREAM

2 cups very cold heavy cream

2 tablespoons confectioners' sugar

YIELD ONE 9-INCH CAKE

Preheat the oven to 350°F. Brush a 9-inch cake pan with oil.

To make the cake: Whisk together the granulated sugar, eggs, and zest in a large bowl until combined. Add the oil, orange blossom water, and juice and whisk until combined.

In a separate bowl, whisk together the flours, baking powder, and salt. Add the flour mixture to the sugar mixture, alternating with the milk, mixing until well combined. Pour the batter into the prepared pan.

Bake for 45 minutes, or until a skewer inserted into the center of the cake comes out clean. Cool the cake on a wire rack before inverting onto a serving plate.

To make the candied oranges: Whisk together the water and granulated sugar in a small saucepan over low heat until the sugar is dissolved. Add the orange slices and poach over low heat for 5 minutes. Set aside to cool.

To make the whipped cream: In the bowl of a stand mixer fitted with the whisk attachment, beat the heavy cream and confectioners' sugar until soft peaks form. Do not overwhip or the cream will become grainy.

To serve, slice the cake into wedges and spoon an orange slice onto the plate, drizzling the cake with the orange syrup. Top with a spoonful of whipped cream.

CARQUINYOLIS DE NARANJA Y ALMENDRAS

Orange and Almond Catalan Biscotti

These twice-baked cookies, flavored with orange and almonds, are a traditional sweet from Catalonia. Known for their satisfyingly crisp and dry texture, *Carquinyolis* are usually enjoyed dipped in a sweet wine, making them the perfect accompaniment to an after-dinner drink or a leisurely coffee.

¼ cup raw, whole almonds, skins on

1 large egg

½ cup sugar

Zest of 1 orange

2 teaspoons fresh orange juice

¾ cup all-purpose flour

1 teaspoon baking powder

YIELD 12 BISCOTTI

Place the almonds in small bowl and add enough water to cover them. Let soak for 30 minutes, or until the skins slide off easily.

Preheat the oven to 325°F. Line a baking sheet with parchment paper.

In a medium bowl, whisk together the egg, sugar, orange zest, and juice. In a separate bowl, combine the flour and baking powder. Using a rubber spatula, add the flour mixture to the egg mixture and mix until combined. Shape into a log and place on the prepared baking sheet. Bake for 15 minutes. Remove from the oven and cool for 10 to 15 minutes.

Using a serrated knife, cut the log crosswise into 1-inch-wide slices. Return to the oven to bake a second time for 10 to 12 minutes, until golden and crisp.

Serve warm or at room temperature after cooled from the second baking. Store in an airtight container at room temperature for up to 2 weeks.

BUNYOLS DE VENT

Catalan Doughnuts

These sweet, fried balls of dough are traditionally flavored with anise liqueur and served on All Saints' Day in Catalonia. *Bunyols* are easy to make and so light and airy (*de vent*, meaning "of wind") that they literally double in size when fried.

Although now eaten to celebrate a Catholic holiday, these delicious treats were made as early as the tenth century by the Jewish people, who called them *bimuelos* and ate them in celebration of Hanukkah.

When cooking the pastries, it is important to keep the temperature of the oil constant. If the oil is not hot enough, the *bunyols* will sink to the bottom of the pan; if the oil is too hot, they cook too quickly and form a crust and will be flat.

---

1 cup whole milk

3½ tablespoons butter

3½ tablespoons granulated sugar

Zest of 1 orange

½ cup all-purpose flour

1½ teaspoons baking powder

⅛ teaspoon kosher salt

2 large eggs

3 teaspoons anise liqueur or fresh orange juice

Neutral vegetable oil for frying

1 cup superfine sugar

¼ cup ground cinnamon

YIELD 24 DOUGHNUTS

In a small saucepan over medium heat, bring the milk, butter, granulated sugar, and zest to a boil. In a small bowl, whisk together the flour, baking powder, and salt. Add the flour mixture to the milk mixture and stir well to combine. Once the dough is smooth, remove from the heat and set aside to cool.

Add the eggs to the cooled dough, one at a time, mixing well with a handheld mixer to combine. Stir in the liqueur. Set aside to rest for 20 to 30 minutes.

In a large sauté pan or skillet with high sides, pour enough oil to fry, but not submerge, the doughnuts. Heat the oil over medium-high heat to 375°F on a candy thermometer.

Using a small ice-cream scoop, form the doughnuts and, using a slotted spoon, carefully lower each ball into the hot oil. Do not overcrowd the pan. Cook, turning occasionally, until puffy and golden in color, 2 to 3 minutes. Transfer to a paper towel–lined plate to cool.

Repeat with the remaining doughnuts.

In a small bowl, stir together the superfine sugar and cinnamon.

Gently roll the doughnuts in the cinnamon-sugar mixture and enjoy warm or at room temperature.

Store in an airtight container at room temperature for a day or two or refrigerate for 3 to 5 days.

MAGDALENAS

Madeleines

These sweet little cakes are modeled after the French madeleine. Their shape is unique, however, as they are baked in mini-muffin pans. Delicate in texture and scented with lemon, these cakes are traditionally served at breakfast, or as an afternoon snack with coffee or hot chocolate.

Vegetable oil for greasing

1 tablespoon granulated sugar, plus more for coating the pan

2 large eggs, lightly beaten

4 tablespoons unsalted butter, melted

Zest of 1 lemon

1½ teaspoons fresh lemon juice

3 tablespoons all-purpose flour

1 teaspoon baking powder

Sparkling sugar for sprinkling

YIELD 12 MADELEINES

Preheat the oven to 350°F.

To prepare the muffin pan, brush each well with vegetable oil and lightly coat with granulated sugar.

In a medium bowl, whisk together the eggs, melted butter, granulated sugar, lemon zest, and juice. Using a rubber spatula, gently fold in the flour and baking powder.

Spoon the mixture into the prepared wells of the pan, filling two-thirds full. Sprinkle the top of each with a pinch of sparkling sugar.

Bake for 15 minutes until golden.

Remove from the oven and immediately turn out of the pan. Serve warm or at room temperature.

Store in an airtight container at room temperature for 1 to 2 days, or in the refrigerator for 5 to 7 days.

TORRIJAS

Cinnamon-Sugar French Toast with Honey

This sweet treat is the Spanish version of French toast. It is traditionally prepared during Lent, but is equally popular for breakfast any time. It is believed to have originated in the Andalusian convents in the fifteenth century as a way to use up stale bread. Choose a bread with a fine crumb and uniform texture, such as a brioche or challah.

3 cups whole milk

½ cup sugar

2 large eggs

2 teaspoons orange zest

Pinch of kosher salt

1 cinnamon stick

Six 3-inch-thick slices brioche, toasted

Neutral vegetable oil for frying

½ teaspoon ground cinnamon

Honey or maple syrup for serving

YIELD 6 SERVINGS

In a large, shallow baking dish, whisk together the milk, ¼ cup of the sugar, the eggs, orange zest, and salt. Add the cinnamon stick. Add the bread and soak until nearly all the liquid is absorbed, about 20 minutes.

Pour 1 inch of the oil into a large sauté pan or skillet and warm over medium heat. Using a slotted spatula, transfer two or three slices of the bread to the pan to fry, cooking on each side for 2 to 3 minutes until puffy and golden brown.

In a shallow dish, mix the remaining ¼ cup sugar and the cinnamon.

Remove the toasted bread from the pan and coat well in the cinnamon-sugar mixture. Transfer to a paper towel-lined plate. Repeat with the remaining bread slices, adding more oil, as needed.

Serve immediately with honey or maple syrup.

CARAMELO DE TURRÓN DE ALMENDRAS

Almond Nougat Candy

Spanish nougat candy dates back to medieval times when the Moors living in Jijona, an area with an abundance of almonds, combined the nuts with honey and pressed the mixture into molds. The candy is now traditionally eaten at Christmas and is made with not only nuts, typically almonds, and honey, but also with sugar and egg whites. It is often flavored with dried fruit, other nuts, and chocolate. There are two types of turrón: turrón Jijona, a chewy candy cut into small, rectangular pieces, and turrón de Alicante, a hard candy broken apart with a mallet for eating. This recipe is for turrón Jijona.

This creamy and chewy candy is a nice addition to a tapas board.

---

2 tablespoons honey

1 cup sugar

1 egg white

Pinch of kosher salt

1 cup toasted Marcona almonds

½ cup thinly sliced dried apricots

YIELD 24 PIECES

Line a 6-by-9-inch baking dish with parchment paper.

In a small saucepan over medium heat, heat the honey and sugar until it reaches the soft-ball stage on a candy thermometer, 235°F.

Meanwhile, in the bowl of a stand mixer fitted with the whisk attachment, beat the egg white with the salt until soft peaks form, about 3 minutes. With the motor running at low speed, slowly drizzle the honey mixture into the beaten egg white until combined. Using a rubber spatula, fold in the almonds and apricots. Transfer the mixture to the prepared baking dish and press it into the pan. Set aside to cool for 3 hours, or overnight.

Slice into small, rectangular-shaped pieces and serve.

Store in an airtight container in the refrigerator for up to 3 weeks.

TARTA DE SANTIAGO

Saint James Cake

The Saint James cake contains almond flour instead of wheat flour, making it a delicious gluten-free treat. It is closely associated with the Camino de Santiago, the walk that passes through Galicia as pilgrims make their way to Santiago de Compostela. Pilgrims have been enjoying this cake since the twelfth century.

Vegetable oil for brushing

2 cups almond flour, plus more for dusting

4 large eggs

1 cup granulated sugar

Zest of 1 lemon

½ teaspoon ground cinnamon

2 tablespoons confectioners' sugar

YIELD ONE 8-BY-8-INCH CAKE

Preheat the oven to 350°F.

Brush an 8-inch square cake pan with vegetable oil and dust with almond flour.

In a medium bowl, whisk together the eggs and granulated sugar until light in color.

In a separate bowl, combine the almond flour, lemon zest, and cinnamon. Add the almond flour mixture to the bowl with the egg mixture and whisk to combine. Transfer the batter to the prepared pan.

Bake for 30 minutes until a skewer inserted into the center comes out clean. Remove from the oven and set aside to cool.

Run a butter knife around the edges of the pan and carefully invert the cake onto a plate. Cut into squares. Sift confectioners' sugar over the top and serve.

Store in an airtight container at room temperature for up to 3 days, or in the refrigerator for 5 to 7 days.

CREMA CATALANA

Catalan Custard

Crema Catalana is traditionally flavored with cinnamon, but delicious alternatives include citrus and espresso. If you don't have a kitchen torch, place the crema Catalana under a broiler until the tops are caramelized.

⅔ cup whole milk

1 vanilla bean, split

1 cinnamon stick

3 wide strips orange peel

½ cup sugar

3 large eggs

YIELD 4 SERVINGS

Preheat the oven to 325°F.

Place the milk, vanilla bean, cinnamon stick, and orange peel in a medium saucepan over medium heat. Cook, just until scalding, then remove from the heat to cool. Strain into a clean bowl, removing the vanilla bean, cinnamon stick, and peels.

In a medium bowl, whisk together ¼ cup of the sugar and the eggs until combined. Whisk in the cooled milk. Divide among four small, oven-proof dishes. Set inside a high-sided baking dish to create a bain-marie. Place in the oven and fill the baking dish two-thirds full of water. Bake until set, about 20 minutes. Carefully remove from the oven and set aside to cool. Transfer to the refrigerator to chill for at least several hours to overnight.

To serve, coat the top of each dish with 1 tablespoon of the remaining sugar. Using a kitchen torch, heat the sugar until it is caramelized and golden.

Serve immediately.

SANGRÍA ESPUMOSA CON POMELO

Sparkling Sangria with Grapefruit

Cava, the sparkling wine of Spain, is made using the same method as champagne. With its citrusy and floral flavors paired with sweet strawberries and freshly squeezed citrus, this sangria is an elegant and refreshing option for summer entertaining.

One 750 ml bottle white wine, such as Albarino

1 cup fresh grapefruit juice

1 grapefruit, halved and cut into ½-inch slices, reserving some for garnish

1 orange, halved and cut into ½-inch slices, reserving some for garnish

8 ounces strawberries, hulled and halved, reserving some for garnish

8 ounces pineapples, diced

One 750 ml bottle Cava or sparkling wine

YIELD 4 TO 6 SERVINGS

In a large pitcher, combine the white wine, grapefruit juice, grapefruit and orange slices, strawberries, and pineapple. Refrigerate for at least 2 hours.

To serve, place several cubes of ice into individual wine glasses and fill halfway with the sangria and fruit. Top with the Cava or sparkling wine. Garnish with the reserved fruit and enjoy.

About Sangria

Grapevines were planted in Spain by the Romans more than two thousand years ago. Since that time, wines made from the grapes have been enjoyed throughout the country. Sangria, served chilled, over ice, is a refreshing alternative to wine during the warm summer months. It is enjoyed throughout Spain, and light versions using a white or rosé wine are preferred. Sangria is a delicious, refreshing, and festive addition to summer entertaining. Feel free to put your own twist on it by mixing together different fruits, herbs, and flowers. Aim for a balance of tart and fruity. Always serve chilled, and take care not to make it overly sweet.

SANGRÍA ROSADO

Rosé Sangria

This jewel-colored sangria is sweetened with juicy summer fruits. The rosé wine produces a light, refreshing, and slightly spicy version of traditional Spanish red sangria. Serve very cold and be sure to allow the fruit to macerate for several hours before serving to soak up all the flavors and soften the fruit.

1 cup sugar

One 750 ml bottle rosé wine

½ cup pomegranate juice

½ cup strawberries, hulled and quartered, plus more for garnish

½ cup raspberries, plus more for garnish

2 red plums, pitted and cut into eighths

1 cup sparkling water

YIELD 4 TO 6 SERVINGS

In a small saucepan, heat 1 cup of water and the sugar over medium heat to make a simple syrup. Boil for 2 minutes. Remove from the heat and set aside to cool.

In a large pitcher, combine the rosé, juice, and fruits. Stir in the cooled simple syrup, cover, and place in the refrigerator to chill for a minimum of 2 hours, or up to overnight.

To serve, add the sparkling water to the pitcher and stir gently to combine. Place several cubes of ice into individual wine glasses and fill with the sangria. Enjoy!

ACKNOWLEDGMENTS

Tapas España is a celebration of Spain, its rich history, and its love of good food and good company.

Over the past thirty years, I've had the privilege of working with and learning from an extraordinary group of creative and talented people. I am endlessly grateful to my community of family and friends, whose shared love of food, wine, curiosity, and celebration has been a constant source of inspiration. Most of all, I would like to thank my husband, Lawrence, and our three children for their excitement, their encouragement, and their appetites.

I am also especially grateful to my editor, Edward Ash-Milby. As a first-time author, I couldn't have asked for a more easygoing, supportive, and enthusiastic partner on this book. Thank you.

INDEX

N

O

P

Q

R

S

ABOUT THE AUTHOR

Catherine Cogliandro Alioto is a classically trained chef, recipe developer, and culinary instructor. She completed her culinary training at Tante Marie's Cooking School in San Francisco and l'ecole Lenôtre in Paris. Catherine has worked with some of the Bay Area's most celebrated restaurants and food companies, and her work has been published in a number of publications including Sunset Books, *Health* magazine, Better Homes and Gardens Books, *Fine Cooking* magazine, and Chronicle Books.

A fourth-generation San Franciscan, Catherine enjoys exploring Northern California markets and restaurants and cooking for family and friends.

She lives in Marin County with her husband and three children.

About the Photographer

Erin Scott is a California food and lifestyle photographer. She is inspired by the beauty of honest food, real people, and the magic of light. When Erin is not behind the camera, you'll often find her cooking or tending to her backyard vegetable patch.

weldon**owen**
an imprint of Insight Editions
P.O. Box 3088
San Rafael, CA 94912
www.weldonowen.com

CEO Raoul Goff
VP Publisher Roger Shaw
Executive Editor Edward Ash-Milby
Assistant Editor Kayla Belser
Managing Editor Michelle Hope
Art Director Megan Sinead Bingham
Production Design Jean Hwang
VP Manufacturing Alix Nicholaeff
Senior Production Manager Joshua Smith
Strategic Production Planner Lina s Palma-Temena

Interior Design Malea Clark-Nicholson
Photography Erin Scott
Food Stylist Lillian Kang

Weldon Owen would also like to thank Margaret Parrish and Mary Cassells.

ISBN: 979-8-88674-355-5

Manufactured in China by Insight Editions
10 9 8 7 6 5 4 3 2 1

Insight Editions, in association with Roots of Peace, will plant two trees for each tree used in the manufacturing of this book. Roots of Peace is an internationally renowned humanitarian organization dedicated to eradicating land mines worldwide and converting war-torn lands into productive farms and wildlife habitats. Roots of Peace will plant two million fruit and nut trees in Afghanistan and provide farmers there with the skills and support necessary for sustainable land use.

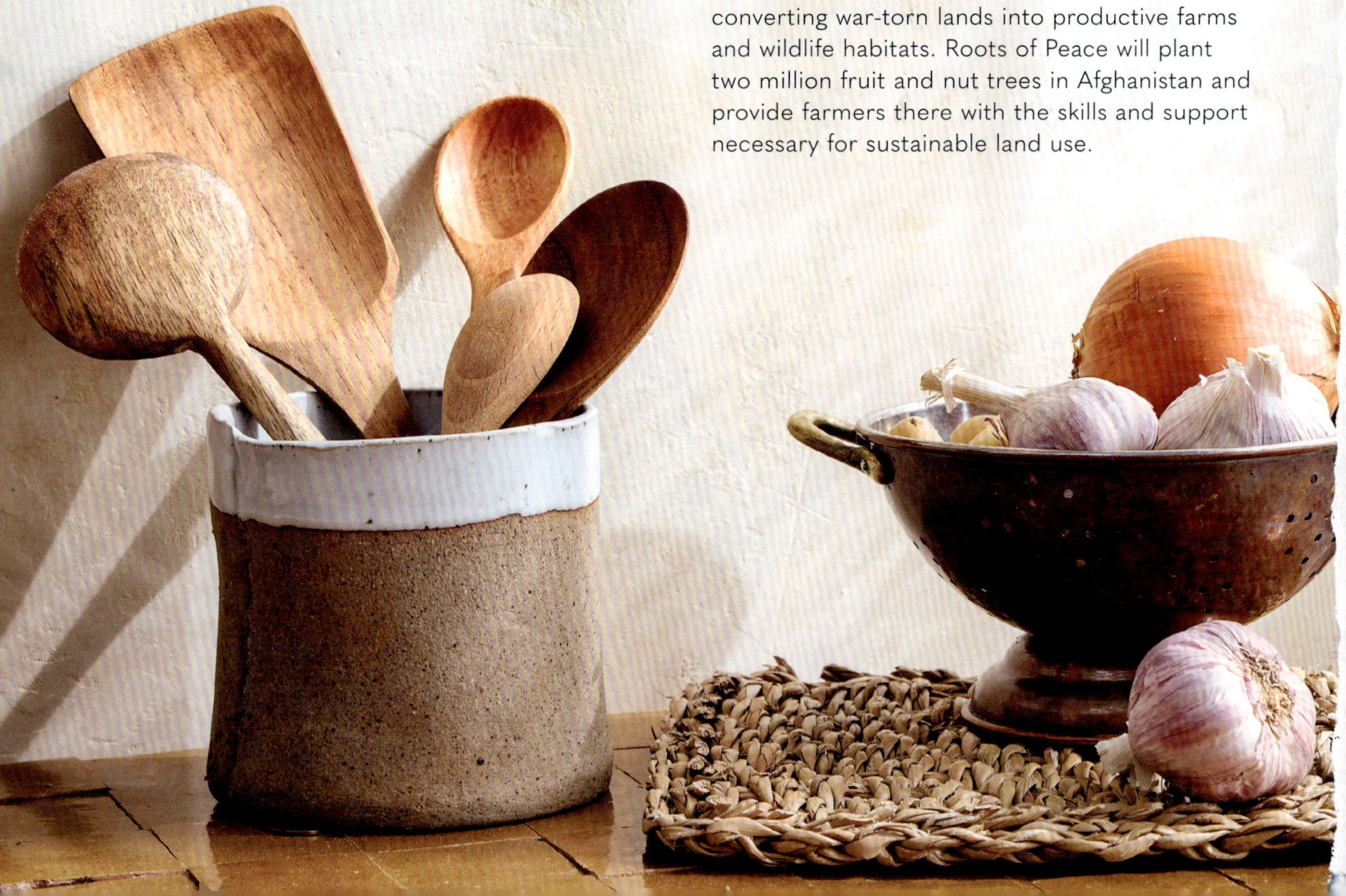